WHAT PEOPLE ARE SAYING ABOUT
MIRACLES FOR VETERANS

Having served in the military (U.S. Navy) for a total of six years, two years at sea on two different warships, I do so appreciate Joan taking the initiative to address the unique needs of those men and women who serve our country in military service. I know this book will minister specifically to those who have served and are currently serving. However, the areas of need that Joan addresses are not limited to those in the military. Anyone who needs a miracle from God can and should claim their miracle by faith. Don't live in pain any longer. Let this book be the inspiration and information you need.

—*Pastor Happy Caldwell*
President, the Victory Television Network (VTN)

I have had the opportunity to read the best of the best books that Christian people have written. Aside from this wonderful opportunity, I read Joan Hunter's book, *Miracles for Veterans*, and learned so much about stress, trauma, suicide, depression, and broken hearts. The bottom line is that *everybody* deals with these issues from the day they are born. If you have ever suffered from a broken heart, an unhealed traumatized childhood, or any issue that caused you to retreat into a life of despair, this book will absolutely change your life. Veterans, to say the least, are one of the most affected groups that this covers. Don't delay, get this book; it will breathe new life into your soul. I recommend it highly because it is coming from a clean vessel!

—*Marilyn Hickey*
Marilyn Hickey Ministries

What a marvelous idea, to not only declare and state the worth of our God as seen through His miraculous activities, but to also honor veterans who have sacrificially given to our nation. As a father whose son is also a veteran, these hold a special place in my heart. My prayer is that not only veterans, but all who need hope will find a new season of faith to continue as the amazing testimonies of these are shared. What God has done for one, He will do again. He is no respecter of persons.

—*Robert Henderson*
Best-selling author, *Courts of Heaven* series

This book tells the truth. *Miracles for Veterans* offers hope, healing, and spiritual recovery for those who have served our country and their families. Joan Hunter understands the very real struggles that our veterans face, but through this anointed book, she offers them a supernatural pathway for God's healing grace to transform their lives. The instruction and prayers contained within this book are not just a theory, but instead, they are practical hands-on tools with remarkable testimonies that prove their effectiveness. If you are a veteran or you know a veteran who needs healing, this book is the answer to your prayers.

—*Joshua Mills*
Best-selling author, *Moving in Glory Realms* and *Seeing Angels*

You are not alone and you are not forgotten! For our amazing veterans who have served our country, God has healing for you. *Miracles for Veterans* is a book like no other. You will find God's solutions for stress and trauma. Every chapter unfolds a new dimension of God's loving grace toward you. Think of it as the cure for the pain that often surfaces from deep within your heart. Read this book and find the love and healing God is offering you. And buy one for a veteran friend. They will thank you for it.

—*Dr. Brian Simmons*
Lead translator, *The Passion Translation*
U.S. Army veteran

It is my pleasure to highly recommend Joan Hunter's newest book to you, *Miracles for Veterans*. I have known Joan for years and ministered alongside her both nationally and internationally. Joan has a plethora of insights in the area of healing—healing is part of her spiritual DNA. But it is not just information with Joan; she sees results of healing in all sorts of areas. Joan is the first person I know of to bring the reality of how trauma can be a catalyst for so many health issues. Trauma can affect us emotionally, mentally, and spiritually as well as physically. In this book, Joan applies the insights the Holy Spirit has given to her about trauma to the experiences and challenges that our veterans face.
You will be amazed and encouraged as you read the testimonies. Veterans are being set free from painful memories, nightmares, and even PTSD. They and their families are being changed. This book is groundbreaking. If there is a *must-read*, this is it. You will be better equipped to help others. For personal challenges, you will get answers and receive hope. Whether a veteran or not, this book is for you.

—*Alan Koch*
Co-founder, Koch Ministries

I have had the pleasure of personally ministering with Joan in various nations and as a speaker in my own church. My observation from watching her minister to people is she's one of the kindest, most caring, genuine ministers I have experienced. This book, *Miracles for Veterans*, is a reflection of her heart toward people who are hurting. My own father was a veteran as were several other family members, so I'm familiar with that world. Joan has been a pioneer in the area of miracles for many years. Her revelation about trauma and erasing memories will be a very powerful and much-needed training tool in helping to set veterans and their families free from hopelessness and depression. It is my absolute pleasure to endorse this book.

—*Carol Koch*
Founder, Children on the Frontlines
Co-founder, Koch Ministries

We've all experienced trauma. Whether you realize it or not, trauma produces negative emotions that can dominate our lives. In *Miracles for Veterans*, Joan Hunter explains that you can overcome your traumatic experiences and be free from whatever negative emotions they've produced. Whether you're a veteran who's been traumatized in the service or you're a civilian who's been wounded by life, there's hope ahead. Joan will show you how to use God's Word to overcome PTSD, broken-heart syndrome, and other conditions that you don't have to live with. The testimonies she tells are compelling, relatable, and easy to connect with. I highly recommend it as a resource for your own personal life or a resource to give to someone in need.

—*Rev. Chris Palmer*
Pastor, Light of Today Ministries; Greek for the Week

Miracles for Veterans is such a powerful and much-needed book to help our veterans and anyone struggling with trauma. I wish this book had been available for my own father, a veteran who suffered from PTSD. Joan Hunter may have written the book of the year for people who are suffering! This is something you will want to buy for all your veteran friends and family.

—*Doug Addison*
Author, *Hearing God Everyday*

In *Miracles for Veterans*, Joan Hunter brings hope, healing, and freedom for those who have served their country in times of war or even times of peace. The teaching from the Word, the personal testimonies, and the powerful prophetic insight will inspire you to receive your miracle!

—*Jane Hamon*
Apostle, Vision Church @ Christian International
Author, *Dreams & Visions; The Deborah Company*

Miracles for Veterans by Joan Hunter is a masterpiece of healing and life for those who have experienced trauma and stress in times of military service. It's a perfect gift of encouragement for friends and family members who have served.

—*Tom Hamon*
Apostle, Vision Church @ Christian International
Author, *7 Anointings for Kingdom Transformation*

MIRACLES FOR
VETERANS

A PATHWAY TO HEALING FOR VETERANS AND THEIR FAMILIES

JOAN HUNTER

WHITAKER
HOUSE

This book is not intended to provide medical advice or to take the place of medical advice and treatment from your personal physician. Readers are advised to consult their own doctors or other qualified health professionals regarding the treatment of their medical problems. Neither the publisher nor the author takes any responsibility for any possible consequences from any treatment, action, or application of medicine, supplement, herb, or preparation to any person reading or following the information in this book. If readers are taking prescription medications, they should consult with their physicians and not take themselves off medicines to start supplementation without the proper supervision of a physician.

MIRACLES FOR VETERANS
A Pathway to Healing for Veterans and Their Families

Joan Hunter Ministries
P.O. Box 111
Tomball, TX 77377
joanhunter.org

ISBN: 978-1-64123-445-0
eBook ISBN: 978-1-64123-446-7
Printed in the United States of America
© 2020 Joan Hunter Ministries

Whitaker House
1030 Hunt Valley Circle
New Kensington, PA 15068
www.whitakerhouse.com

Library of Congress Cataloging-in-Publication Data (Pending)

1 2 3 4 5 6 7 8 9 10 11 ⽊ 27 26 25 24 23 22 21 20

DEDICATION

To my father, Charles E. Hunter,
who served in the U.S. Air Force during
World War II, and to all of the men and women
who have served our country
as well as those still serving today.

Charles E. Hunter

CONTENTS

ACKNOWLEDGMENTS

A special thank-you to all who contributed to this book, sharing their own amazing stories of their incredible journeys.

There is one amazing woman who helped me make this book happen: Naida Johnson, RN, CWS, FCCWS. Her expertise in compiling all of the testimonies and the editing are beyond words. She prays as she does the editing for the power of God to go into each word. She is a godsend to me, my parents, and everyone who reads this book. Her devotion to God and all she does for Him shines brightly. And she has been an amazing friend for over thirty-five years.

INTRODUCTION

Life is a series of steps toward your destiny. Each step you take is your choice. Even the direction you go is a choice. Reading this book will give you many chances to either make informed choices as you learn from the experiences of others…or continue to stumble through life trying your own way.

Let me use an analogy that played out in my life when I moved to a new home a few years ago. Moving is indeed a stress-filled time of life; however, it is also exciting as you anticipate a new chapter in your journey. Since I am traveling most of the time, I had to make specific, detailed plans for those who would assist me in the move. Of course, this added to my personal stress level.

With such a mountain of work ahead of me, friends and family were scheduled to assist with carrying, packing, and unpacking. I needed their help because I couldn't possibly do all the work by myself.

One person obtained the packing boxes that were the right shape and size for the move, and scattered these boxes around our house. We made sure everyone had packing tape and markers in their pockets. Every box had to be labeled and marked for the rooms where they would go in the new house. I designed a map to show where things should be placed, whether for decoration or by usefulness and function.

Preparing to move into that perfect new home, my decisions also included purchasing necessities. I also had to unpack the old—the boxes that were in storage, closets, and the attic since our last move. I had to prioritize what we would need or use in the near future, what could be put on a shelf for later, or what we might need as back-ups.

Items that had lost their usefulness were donated to someone who could use and appreciate them while broken things were sent out to be repaired or discarded. Even discards are considered treasures by some and can be renewed and repurposed.

WHAT CHANGES CAN YOU MAKE?

Now, let's apply this to why you picked up this book to read. Everyone has issues, whether physical, mental, emotional, or financial. How are you going to change *your* situation?

First, you are going to identify where you are now and where you want to be. You will find resources, like this book, to assist you in making good decisions toward your future.

You can blindly stumble along or you can learn from others' experiences through books, tapes, or media. Find others to help you with prayer, communication, wise counsel, and God-given wisdom. When you have learned as much as you can, you move forward with wisdom.

The most important thing you must carry in your arsenal is God's Word. Most phones have the Bible app on them, so let me ask you a question: if your phone was taken away, do you know enough of His Word to carry you through difficult circumstances? Trying to navigate this life without His Word is like going into battle without any weapons or protection.

Let Him have His way in you. Please join with me in this salvation prayer:

Father, I know You are in charge of everything. Thank You for my life and all that I am. I have made mistakes so many times. Please forgive me for ignoring You and not following Your plan for my life. Only You can heal me. Father, I accept Jesus into my life and want Your Holy Spirit to guide me from this day forward. As I read this book, open my heart and mind to hear You and follow You! In Jesus's name. Amen!

Before you were even born, God decided where You, His child, should be placed on earth to be the most functional and beneficial to His work at a particular time. He places people strategically for today's plans. He may see one person's potential, but He puts them on the back burner or shelf or pew.

People who have completed their assignment may move on to help someone else. Their assignment in the present is over. Their gifts are needed elsewhere.

The broken need to sit under further teaching in order to get healthy and grow to the level where God can again use their services. Unfortunately, some choose to be discarded into the enemy's camp. However, as long as there is just one prayer and just one person who discovers that discarded, unwanted soul, there is always hope of restoration and reconciliation to the Father.

GOD HAS PLANS FOR YOU

Now, can you apply this analogy in your situation? Look, learn, and apply what you read in this book. Cling to the positives and discard your previous unproductive choices. God has a plan for your life. Your previous experiences are meant to prepare you for the next chapter of your life. Whether the stress was positive or negative, God can use *you*! He will use *all* of you for His purpose. He will turn all negative stressful and traumatic experiences into something good.

Please have an open heart and mind as you continue. Some stories in this book may make you cry while others will make you smile. All of this information will prepare you to walk in total victory and help others to do the same. God is always faithful and He hears your heart's cry. Open your arms to your Father's love right now and let that love heal you—body, mind, spirit, emotions, and finances.

Believe this is the day for your breakthrough, your *victory*. Everyone has bad days. Some have bad months, but there is SONshine coming for everyone. Just like a new recruit has to go through basic training or boot camp in order to advance in rank and responsibility, everyone has to do the same in God's military. Learn the offensive thrust that carries you to the frontlines and through the enemy's defenses.

Get prepared. Stay prepared. Don't run away or get trampled on. Don't be left behind.

Our motto is PUSH: Pray Until Something Happens!

Be on the offensive and go after God. He is the Commander in Chief of these end-time armed forces!

God is waiting for *you*, so hang on. He is calling *you* to attention.

It is time to *charge*!

PART 1:

ISSUES

★ 1 ★
STRESS AND TRAUMA

Everyone has their own definition of stress and trauma, depending on their previous experiences. Let's examine these two conditions so we will understand what each actually means in the context of this discussion.

POSITIVE AND NEGATIVE STRESS

To varying degrees, all of us experience feelings of stress on a daily basis. This is the body reacting to a *challenge* that could be either physical or psychological.

Feelings of stress can be either positive (excitement) or negative (threatening). Stress can increase your awareness of your surroundings as well as your blood pressure and your heart rate. Winning the lottery, receiving a promotion, and planning a vacation are all examples of positive stress.

The main emphasis of this book is negative stress. Physical stress is obvious each time you flex or extend a muscle. Mental stress can range from reading information—such as a low balance in your checkbook or a negative comment on social media—to facing a threatening situation. The latter stage of stress lets you know you are being approached by something with the potential to harm you or someone close to you. Your past experiences will enable you to quickly evaluate the situation and decide what to do next: confront, remove, or run. Medical journals often call this survival physiology the fight-or-flight response. It's a typical reaction meant to protect a person from harm.

Traumatic stress or extreme fear triggers many changes in the body to help you defend against danger or avoid it. Nearly everyone will experience a range of reactions with traumatic stress, yet most people recover from initial symptoms naturally.

STRESS STARTS AT BIRTH

We experience stress when we are born—and perhaps even before then, in the womb. Any traumatic stress that the pregnant mother goes through will also affect her unborn child. As any mother can tell you, giving birth is not the most pleasant experience in the world, even though the memory of the pregnancy, contractions, labor pains, and pushing will fade with the joy of holding their newborn child. Medical professionals claim that babies don't remember their traumatic entry into this world—the pulling, kicking, and twisting they endure making their way through the birth canal. We all think babies are so delicate, without stopping to consider how much effort it took for them to be born.

You can see from this one very common example that stress can be both good and bad. Without the stress in our lives, we do not grow, develop, or mature into a productive, useful, wise adult meant to aid others on their bumpy journey through life. Babies continue to experience stress and can only wail in discomfort when they are hungry or need new diapers. Their parents' arrival and comforting arms lower that stress level and unconsciously teach the baby how to deal with the basic stress levels of their new world.

As anything grows and develops, it learns how to survive. Even a young tree has to learn which direction to grow in order to reach food and water. A young root banging against a rock will never overcome its stress level. Moving an inch will change its route to an easier path that yields success.

Nothing on earth is exempt from stress, but we will concentrate on what affects our human lives and how to manage the stress faced on a daily basis. A certain degree of healthy stress is great. It moves you toward victory and success. On the other hand, uncontrolled, negative stress can become chronic with undesirable changes in every area of your life.

CONSEQUENCES OF CHRONIC STRESS

Physical, mental, and psychological issues can develop from chronic stress, leading to permanent changes in physiological, emotional, and behavioral areas. In fact, people can have more pain from long-lasting emotional problems than from a fractured bone.

Experiencing chronic stress as a child can have lifelong effects on a person's responses to stress later in life. Even a relationship conflict lasting over one month can contribute to a physical illness.

Acute stress typically does not impose a burden on young, healthy individuals. However, chronic stress in already compromised people may have long-term effects that are detrimental to their ongoing health.

Chronic stress can impact the cardiovascular system, leading to hypertension and other complications related to some common heart diseases.

Some people turn to alcohol, food, or drugs to temporarily relieve the stress. Unfortunately, alcohol and drug use or dependence often develop into other serious abuse situations that can increase stress levels both for the individuals involved and their families.

Children growing up in a home environment involving serious marital discord, alcoholism, the use of illegal drugs, or child abuse experience chronic stress that can impact their physical, mental, emotional, and spiritual growth. Prenatal life, infancy, childhood, and adolescence are critical periods during which the child's vulnerability to stress is particularly high. Early childhood experiences should not be ignored.

IMMUNE SYSTEM AFFECTED

God made our bodies with the amazing ability to regenerate cells and heal themselves. Stress and trauma are the hidden factors that can secretly erode our body's immune system and its ability to heal and remain healthy. If you do not learn to deal with stress and trauma properly, your body loses its ability to resist illness and you become a magnet for disease.

Stress that enhances function such as strength training or other positive challenges is considered both useful and healthy. Think of your favorite successful athlete. They have spent countless stressful hours in order to accomplish their goals. Being strongly encouraged to improve or reach seemingly unrealistic goals can cause increased stress that can also push an employee to new levels of ability and talent.

Keeping the house clean, food on the table, and the children dressed and well-behaved is not an easy task. Earning enough money to pay for the family's needs can also be quite a responsibility. Everything you do has its own level of stress that you need to manage and overcome on a regular basis.

BEING IN DISTRESS

Persistent stress that is not considered helpful is called *distress*, which can lead to anxiety, withdrawal, depression, or other negative behaviors. Any alarming experience, either real or imagined, can trigger a stress response and cause distress emotionally, physically, or physiologically.

Being physically, sexually, or mentally abused, children can have all kind of stressful issues throughout their lives. Usually, these problems are hidden because of shame and fear. Often, these hidden stressful events come exploding out of the person in very strange displays of trauma to themselves and others.

Here's a very simple example: if someone panics at high elevations, such as looking over the edge of a cliff or a tall building, chances are, they fell or were injured during a previous fall. Often, the cause may not be readily identified, but the effects can last a lifetime.

Some people almost get addicted to the excitement and stimulation of acute stress. Think about the people who love to bungee jump off a high bridge or parachute from miles above the earth. Race car drivers and rodeo cowboys who ride bucking bulls frequently put themselves in a position of dangerous stress. Even a very realistic, scary movie can cause the fight-or-flight response. These folks love the excitement and return again and again to these high-stress events.

SYMPTOMS OF STRESS

Stress can affect all aspects of your life, including your emotions, behaviors, thinking ability, and physical health. No part of the body is immune. But because people handle stress differently, symptoms of stress can vary.

Symptoms can be vague and may resemble those caused by medical conditions. They may also occur in any number of combinations. Anyone who identifies with these very common symptoms should consult their doctor.

Physical Symptoms

Physical symptoms of anxiety and stress include, but are not limited to, cardiovascular problems such as abnormal heart rhythm, elevated blood pressure, rapid heartbeat, heart disease or stroke, diabetes, trouble sleeping, upset stomach, chest pain, and headaches. People coping with stress and anxiety may also suffer from low energy, muscular aches and pains, frequent infections and colds, excess sweating, and dry mouth or difficulty swallowing. Diarrhea, acid reflux, gastritis, indigestion, nausea, and constipation can occur when the stomach is upset due to anxiety and stress.

People who are worried, stressed, or anxious may grind their teeth or clench their jaw and experience ringing in the ear, changes in appetite, and nervous behaviors such as pacing, fidgeting, and nail-biting. Stress and anxiety can also cause shaking, faintness, dizziness or lightheaded sensations, trembling of the hands and lips, and cold or sweaty feet and hands.

Without managing or treating their stress or anxiety, some may experience sexual dysfunction, a loss of sexual desire or sexual ability, menstrual problems, skin and hair problems, headaches, tremors, cold or sweaty hands, unexplained allergy attacks, and unexplained weight gain or loss. Long-term stress and anxiety can also lead to mental health illnesses such as depression or personality disorders.

Emotional Symptoms

Emotional symptoms of stress include becoming easily agitated, experiencing uncontrollable anger, fighting, feelings of frustration, or moodiness. Some may feel overwhelmed, unable to relax, lonely, or depressed. People may avoid contact with others, have low self-esteem, and be pessimistic or see only the negative aspects of their life. Disorganization is another symptom of someone suffering from the emotional aspects of stress.

Behavioral Symptoms

Behavioral symptoms of stress include changes in appetite, procrastinating and avoiding responsibilities, increased use of alcohol, drugs, or tobacco products, nail-biting, fidgeting, and pacing.

CONSEQUENCES OF LONG-TERM STRESS

A little stress every now and then is not something to be concerned about. Ongoing, chronic stress, however, can cause or exacerbate many serious health problems.

You may wonder why I included stress problems related to children in a book about healing for veterans. The truth is, if a young person hasn't learned how to handle their stressful issues, their repressed anger and frustrations can emerge later in destructive and damaging ways.

When eligible to join the military, young men and women sign on the dotted line. Yes, I realize most have noble goals of serving their country and keeping us safe. I commend each member of our armed forces and gratefully thank them for their service.

I want to address the few who serve because one of their top desires is learning how to fight. Their pent-up feelings of youthful stress and trauma may emerge into violent, uncontrolled behavior. They may learn to handle explosives and enjoy destroying things. Learning to kill is acceptable and expected. War is not fun or pleasant; however, some servicemen absolutely love that life.

Then they come home. The government had instructed and ordered certain obedient behaviors when they were fighting; however, upon discharge, those learned behaviors are now against the law. Servicemen and women are discharged from the service and have to adapt to normal life. Violence was once acceptable and expected, but now it's considered bad behavior and totally unacceptable. Instead of a commendation and appreciation, the discharged veteran may face jail or incarceration because of uncontrolled behaviors.

Transition back to peaceful life is not easy or universal. Long-lived stress and trauma, often from youth, has to be dealt with. To my knowledge, there is no specific government program to assist in this difficult, long-term transition.

People using wisdom can and will avoid stressful experiences that increase their blood pressure to dangerous levels. Once you experience such stimulating events, you also must learn how to cool down and control lasting effects. For instance, by just watching movies or TV reports depicting traumatic and dangerous events, some people can have nightmares for years. This is especially true for young children exposed to dangerous experiences, whether on the screen or in real life.

Sometimes, people carry guilt and blame themselves for the physical, emotional, or verbal abuse that they experienced when they were children. This is false responsibility that requires prayer and healing so they can be set free.

DIFFERENT DEGREES OF TRAUMA

When you hear the word *trauma*, you will probably think of physical injury such as a car accident, burns from a fire, or being attacked, shot, stabbed, or beaten by another individual. Of course, falls, sports injuries, and other accidents are also included in this category. Trauma centers and emergency rooms are located throughout the country. The former, however, specialize specifically in the treatment of traumatic event injuries such as broken bones, cracked skulls, internal damage, or other life-threatening wounds requiring immediate treatment or surgical repair.

Trauma includes any serious injury to a person, often resulting from violence or an accident. Hitting your thumb with a hammer or getting burned by a splash of scalding hot water can also be considered trauma even though most people don't run to an emergency room doctor for help with such a small injury. Falling off a bicycle, being thrown off a horse, or falling out of a tree can be traumatic for one child while another can find it funny as they brush themselves off and repeat the activity again and again. Dangerous sports activities can cause the same reaction.

Whether you participate or watch intense sporting events like football, ice hockey, or racing, your heartrate and blood pressure increase. The news stories of school shootings, huge fires, murders, explosions, hurricanes, flooding, war casualties, and plane crashes all keep millions of people glued to the TV. These traumatic events may or may not directly involve you or someone you know, but they do affect you in one way or another.

Major physical injury trauma involving the loss of consciousness or brain function requires immediate medical attention.

NON-PHYSICAL TRAUMA

Psychological trauma is a type of emotional damage that occurs as a result of a severely distressing event. It may take years to resolve this trauma. Spiritual, emotional, and mental trauma must also be considered. These areas often overlap with each other as well as with physical trauma.

Rarely is there one type of trauma without at least one or more of the other forms of it in a situation. Trauma is one of the biggest doors that can open up our lives and our bodies to sickness.

Severe post-traumatic stress disorder (PTSD) has physical symptoms also. A medical professional who does not conduct a thorough interview with an affected client may not connect the PTSD with the symptoms. I have seen this trauma response come out with chronic diseases such as fibromyalgia.

Disguising or hiding symptoms often becomes second nature to PTSD clients. For example, veterans are supposed to be so macho and strong, they don't want to admit to their inability to handle stress and trauma. Their commitment to and experiences in military service was their identity. Returning to everyday life becomes its own form of stress. Their urge to seek excitement and danger also contribute to this problem. (*For more on PTSD, see chapter three.*)

Some medical specialists don't believe stress or trauma have any relationship to disease. Thank God, someone has recognized this situation and responded with a plan to confirm this relationship. Because the effects of trauma on a human being are extensive, but not yet specifically identified, billions of dollars have been assigned to thirty-five scientists to study this problem. It's hoped that this will lead to a better understanding of prevention and treatment. (*See Steps to Healing, chapter sixteen.*)

BE AWARE OF CHOICES

Just watching too much negative news can trigger depression and anxiety as worry and fear accelerate. Following a reported shooting on the news recently, a loud noise in a shopping mall caused mass panic and fear. Please use wisdom and be aware of your surroundings. If you are a police officer, firefighter, or serving in the armed forces, you are trained as a first responder and will run toward the problem. Anyone else should attempt to stay calm, assess the situation, and quickly seek safety.

Please realize that the environment where you choose to spend time will affect you positively or negatively. You usually have a choice. For example, avoid being outside in bad areas of town in the dark of night or alone in a deserted area. Make sure you have enough gas in your vehicle and keep doors locked. Keep your cell phone nearby. Use wisdom. Pray and trust God's direction. Children must develop trust in their parents and follow their instructions. Adults have to make a wise choice to protect children or other incapacitated or helpless people in danger. If you follow God's advice, you will pray unceasingly and He will give you the right answer as to the safest action to take in a situation.

Even though it may bring up unpleasant memories, think back to your bad experiences. List them in black and white. This list will be used later during the healing phase of this book.

YOUR LIST OF EXPERIENCES

_____

_____

_____

_____

_____

_____

_____

_____

2

CHRONIC ISSUES AND TRAUMA TRANSFERENCE

Traumatic stress can lead to many chronic illnesses. Fibromyalgia, chronic pain or fatigue, severe anxiety or depression, autoimmune problems, and digestive problems such as irritable bowel syndrome and Crohn's disease are only a few of the chronic physical problems that can be exacerbated or caused by traumatic stress.

The traumatized body has difficulty controlling the fight-or-flight reaction to stress. The constant stress triggers long-standing chronic illnesses. The more trauma a child experiences, the higher incidence of chronic illnesses in later life. Positive affirmations may help, but they don't get to the cellular level.

Research shows that stressful environments that are unsafe and unpredictable cause a person to be overly cautious, nervous, and jumpy. This condition can become toxic to a person's system. Body systems can shut down. Normal reactions, growth, and healing freeze.

About 63 percent of white, middle-class America have suffered from traumatic experiences and this number climbs among other ethnic groups. Trauma has actually reached epidemic levels in the United States.

When traumatic stress occurs, the first reaction is to run; however, a person may not be able to escape the situation, so their oxygen levels and metabolism may fall. If the traumatic stress persists, organs can also shut down as the person goes into survival mode. High levels of trauma can contribute to ongoing anxiety in the future.

Learn the symptoms of trauma and establish a safe environment. If you can't get to the cause of a particular disease problem, persistent, chronic traumatic stress may be involved.

Because trauma is stored in the nervous system, long-standing discomfort or numbing pain may be psychological. Don't just pass it off. Attempt to find out why it's there and tell it to leave in Jesus's name!

TRAUMA TRANSFERENCE

Every traumatic experience affects everything in a person's life. The way you think, learn, feel, react, and speak are changed. A trauma victim needs help to deal with and process their emotions. The images, feelings, and sensations are imprinted and stored in the body's cellular memory.

In times of high stress or emotional upheaval, a trauma victim's responses are usually not normal. The body's fight-or-flight response kicks in and they may become violent physically or verbally. They can be reliving the initial experience with the same emotions, such as fear. This is one way to transfer the initial traumatic experience to someone else. Even talking too much about what happened initially can instill fear into another. This reactive trauma can manifest in anger, rage, sadness, fear, shame, loneliness, or abandonment.

A person can suffer from trauma merely by hearing about or seeing someone else's traumatic experience. Take, for example, an elementary school student who is asked to interview a grandparent and write an essay. While the child asks him questions, Grandpa's stories about war become very gruesome and scary. Add violent TV programs and a few nightmares to the mix and the child also becomes a trauma victim. She now feels Grandpa's pain and thinks adulthood means living in constant danger.

First responders, whether on the battlefield or city streets, are often exposed to violent destruction and mangled bodies. Many people not in those fields or in the medical profession cannot even handle the sight of blood. For them, just witnessing the results of a serious accident can trigger a traumatic response. The blood, gore, and smell of reality is much different than the make-up and special effects seen in movies or on TV. They can faint when they have to provide a small blood sample during a routine checkup because it's too traumatic for them.

WE ALL SUFFER FROM TRAUMA

Everyone is a trauma victim to a certain extent. Think for a minute. What upsets you? What triggers a serious response? A specific sound, a certain smell, or a touch? During a flashback, people may feel the same emotion they did during a traumatic event. Flashbacks may occur more often with any high-stress situation.

Pray about it. Let God show you what brings back those traumatic memories so you can be prepared to handle them. Find a counselor, if necessary. Stop the trauma before it gets transferred to a family member or friend. Continue to read this book to discover how to eliminate the cellular memory that causes the replay of a traumatic event. *(See Steps to Healing, chapter sixteen.)*

I ministered to the grandchild of a Jewish Holocaust survivor. All she knew was her grandparents had survived that horrific event. No one shared stories or talked about what had happened in the German concentration camps, yet this woman could give specific details about what her grandparents had experienced.

Another young woman could explain what had happened to her mother before she was born. Mom, who had been beaten and raped, had never told her story to anyone, but her daughter knew details that no one else knew.

Researchers are now studying trauma transference, including the possibility of transference through DNA. The person involved may have difficulty determining whether their memories are from the past or present.

3

POST-TRAUMATIC STRESS DISORDER (PTSD)

Post-traumatic stress disorder, or PTSD, is a medical diagnosis for a specific anxiety disorder. It can develop after exposure to a stressful traumatic event that can cause negative emotional reactions many years later. Combat, acts of violence, and physical injury from rape, mugging, disasters, accidents, kidnapping, and other horrific experiences are obvious forms of trauma. Yet there are many other kinds of trauma that may leave emotional scars that can lead to PTSD. In addition to severe anxiety, PTSD can even cause disability.

If you are a family member, do you recognize the following issues in your loved one?

SIGNS AND SYMPTOMS

Every person who has experienced trauma has the potential to developing chronic or short-term PTSD. Not everyone with PTSD has been through a dangerous event. Some other experiences, such as the unexpected death of a loved one, can also cause PTSD.

Symptoms usually begin within three months of the traumatic incident, but they sometimes don't appear until many years afterward. Symptoms must last more than a month and interfere with relationships or work to be considered PTSD.

The course of the illness varies. Some people recover within six months, while others have symptoms that last much longer. The condition can become chronic and last a lifetime.

People with PTSD may feel stressed or frightened even when they are not in any danger. PTSD is often called the silent killer of military personnel because many former servicemen and women commit suicide to escape this tormenting condition.

Anyone diagnosed with PTSD will have one or more of the following symptoms:

- Flashbacks—reliving the trauma over and over, including physical symptoms such as a racing heart or excessive sweating
- Nightmares about the event or frightening thoughts; difficulty sleeping
- Staying away from places, events, or objects that are reminders of the traumatic experience
- Avoiding thoughts or feelings related to the traumatic event
- Being easily startled; becoming upset or overreacting when reminded of a previous stressful situation or person
- Irritable, angry outbursts; feeling tense or on edge
- Trouble remembering key features of previous events
- Negative thoughts about oneself or the world
- Distorted feelings such as guilt or self-blame
- Loss of interest in enjoyable activities
- Avoid conflict
- Feel alone even when with other people
- Hallucinations about a traumatic event
- Feelings of helplessness, fear, or horror when witnessing or experiencing a life-threatening event, or watching scary movies or videos
- Overreacting to seeing, sensing, or smelling something that specifically brings back memories of a negative stressful event
- A problem maintaining friendships
- Feelings of depression; loss of interest in normal, daily activities
- Requires alcohol or drugs to get through the day
- Memory gaps when thinking about childhood

Re-experiencing symptoms may cause problems in a person's everyday routine. The symptoms can start from the person's own thoughts and feelings. Words, objects, people, or situations become reminders of the event and may trigger symptoms. Avoidance may cause a person to change his or her personal routine. For example, after a bad car accident, a person who usually drives may avoid driving or riding in a car. PTSD symptoms can make the person feel angry with any additional stress. These symptoms may also make it hard to sleep, eat, or concentrate.

It is natural to feel these symptoms after a dangerous event. Symptoms related to an acute stress disorder, or ASD, may disappear after a few weeks. When the symptoms last more than a month, affect one's functional ability, and not due to other causes, PTSD may be diagnosed by a psychologist or psychiatrist. Some people with PTSD don't show any symptoms for weeks or months. PTSD is often accompanied by one or more of the other anxiety disorders.

RISK FACTORS

Not everyone who experiences a traumatic event will develop PTSD. Symptoms of PTSD are more likely to occur if a person has any of the following risk factors:

1. Previous traumatic experiences because stress of trauma can have a cumulative effect and a new traumatic experience can exacerbate the negative effects of the previous trauma.

    a. Natural disasters such as fires, earthquakes, tornados, and hurricanes

    b. Interpersonal violence like rape, child abuse, or the suicide of a loved one or friend

    c. Involvement in a serious car accident or workplace accident

    d. Acts of violence such as an armed robbery, war, or terrorism

2. Family history of anxiety, PTSD, or depression. This can include trauma transference syndrome or transgenerational syndrome. Some people develop PTSD after a friend or family member experiences danger or harm.

3. Having a history of mental illness or substance abuse can interfere with a person's ability to cope with the added stress of a traumatic event.

4. History of poor coping skills. A lowered level of psychological functioning may diminish self-control. They may blame themselves rather than the stress.

5. Lack of social support: these people are more vulnerable to stress and at a higher risk for PTSD following trauma. They need positive social and family relationships to handle the psychological effects.

6. Ongoing stress. After a stressful event, such as loss of a loved one, pain and injury, or loss of a job or home, resulting in feelings of horror, helplessness, or extreme fear.

7. Living through more than one dangerous event or trauma.

8. Childhood trauma.

9. Seeing another person seriously wounded or killed; or seeing a dead body.

10. Sexual dysfunction.

11. Extreme alertness; always on the lookout for warnings of potential danger.

ONGOING STRESS CAN TRIGGER PTSD

Events of ongoing stress can increase the effect or likelihood of risk for PTSD, which can happen to anyone at any age. Some are able to recover within six months while others may battle the symptoms for many years. Symptoms vary in frequency and intensity.

According to the National Center for PTSD, about seven or eight out of every one hundred people will experience PTSD at some point in their lives. Women are more likely to develop PTSD than men and there may be a genetic or transgenerational factor involved.

The diagnosis of post-traumatic stress disorder was obviously a serious condition long before the medical community recognized it in the 1970s following the Vietnam War. PTSD was considered a severe and ongoing emotional reaction to an extreme psychological trauma often associated with military personnel, police officers, and other emergency personnel. Initially, it was believed that the stressor involved a threat to your life, seeing the actual death of someone else, or experiencing a serious physical injury or a threat to your physical or psychological well-being.

Eventually, the diagnosis of PTSD was expanded to include other triggers, such as severe devastation, abusive environments, and the experiences of first responders. In some cases, people can suffer from PTSD because of profound psychological and emotional trauma without any actual physical harm or threat. Often, however, the two are combined.

PHYSICAL HEALTH AND PTSD

Medical literature indicates a potential link between PTSD and physical health. Veterans, active duty military personnel, first responders, civilians, firefighters, and adolescents who have reported PTSD symptoms are more likely to also have a greater number of health issues, often with poor outcomes.

The National Center for PTSD and other laboratories around the world are studying this situation. The experience of trauma can cause neurochemical changes in the brain that may have biological, psychological, and behavioral effects on one's health. MRI and CT scans have revealed that trauma actually changes both the structure and the function of the brain. Research also shows that these neurochemical changes may relate to abnormalities in cardiovascular and hormonal functions, as well as increased susceptibility to infections and abnormal immune disorders associated with PTSD.

Potentially traumatic events can be caused by a singular occasion or from ongoing, relentless stresses. A potentially traumatic event is more prone to leave an individual with longer-lasting emotional and psychological trauma if:

+ The individual was unprepared for the event
+ It occurred suddenly and unexpectedly, such as the death of a loved one
+ The person felt powerless to prevent the event
+ The event occurred repeatedly, such as child abuse
+ It involved extreme cruelty
+ It occurred during the childhood years
+ It involved divorce or the breakup of a significant relationship
+ The person experienced significant humiliation
+ The event was major surgery, severe illness, serious hospitalization
+ It included major falls or injuries
+ The person was diagnosed with a life-threatening or disabling condition

TRIGGERED BY POWERFUL, UPSETTING EVENTS

Potentially traumatic events are defined as events that are both powerful and upsetting intrusions of a person's daily life. Generally speaking, potentially traumatic events involve a major threat to one's psychological and physical well-being. They may threaten the life of that person or one of their loved ones.

For some individuals, such events have little or no impact; for others, they cause significant distress. How a potentially traumatic event affects a person may be related to their mental or physical health, past traumatic experiences, the presence of coping skills, and the level of their social and emotional support during the event.

It's important to note that other, less severe but ultimately stress-inducing situations can also trigger traumatic reactions in some men and women.

The symptoms of psychological trauma may be increasingly severe and last longer. This may be the result of the traumatic event, lack of emotional support, past and present stressors, personality issues, and coping mechanisms.

PSYCHOLOGICAL TRAUMA

Some of the most common symptoms of psychological trauma may include the following:

+ Overwhelming fear
+ Obsessive and compulsive behaviors
+ Detachment from other people and emotions
+ Emotional numbing
+ Depression
+ Guilt, especially if one lived while others perished
+ Shame
+ Emotional shock
+ Disbelief
+ Irritability
+ Anger

EFFECTS OF UNTREATED PSYCHOLOGICAL TRAUMA

Many people live for years with the symptoms of emotional and psychological trauma as their world grows steadily smaller. The effects of untreated psychological trauma can be devastating and infiltrate nearly every aspect of an individual's life.

Some of the most common effects of untreated trauma include:

+ Substance abuse or alcoholism
+ Sexual problems or dysfunction
+ Inability to maintain healthy close and appropriate relationships
+ Hostility or constant arguments with loved ones
+ Social withdrawal
+ Constant feelings of being threatened
+ Self-destructive or impulsive behaviors
+ Uncontrollable reactive thoughts
+ Inability to make healthy occupational or lifestyle choices
+ Compulsive behavioral patterns
+ Feelings of depression, shame, hopelessness, or despair
+ Feeling ineffective or feeling as though one is permanently damaged
+ Loss of former belief systems

Grief, sadness, depression, or anxiety are known to trigger further added or exacerbated stress. Any major change in one's life can cause stress, along with unrealistic expectations and fear. Each person experiences different triggers related to previous events.

The National Center for PTSD reports that five out of ten women experience a traumatic event in their lifetime and the most common trauma for women and children is sexual assault or abuse. Another study found that one in four women and one in ten men experienced sexual abuse as a child. It is logical to say sexual abuse without adequate support or treatment could cause long-term trauma.

A survivor may feel like their heart has been ripped out of their chest. They may believe that they deserved to be treated with abuse and disrespect, or that they caused the problem in the first place. Some children believe that abuse is a form of love. (*See part two for testimonies of PTSD survivors.*)

4

DEPRESSION

Depression is a mental disorder marked by persistent sadness, severe dejection, inactivity, and feeling worthless, hopeless, and inadequate. This includes a lack of energy, interest, and desire.

The research involved in studying depression and its causes, treatments, and medications can be overwhelming. So many people are suffering from this common attack from the enemy. It sneaks in and settles on your shoulder. Then it slowly convinces you that it is your friend as it whispers destruction and death into your ears, mind, and heart.

When a person finds they can no longer do what they used to do, it is quite common for signs of depression to manifest. Whether older, injured, discharged from the service, or retired, you find your abilities and opportunities are very different. Perhaps you once were a CEO, a teacher, a nurse, or a decorated member of the armed forces. Now suddenly, your identity has dissolved into something you don't recognize. The familiar proverbial door has closed and the door to depression can swing wide open.

I want to share my heart with you because depression tried to sneak into my life. I refused to let it stay in my heart or my mind. I want to help you get completely free of any form of depression. You may read this entire teaching and think freedom just can't be that simple. Well, you know what? I encourage you to continue to the very end. If you really want to get free of depression, you *will* be free. This is not just a little bandage. I don't want you to just learn how to live *with* it. I want you to be completely free from depression so that it never visits you again.

UNDERSTANDING THE CAUSE IS KEY

When people talk about depression, they often explain that their doctor has given them medications to balance chemicals in their body. That may help temporarily, but I want those chains broken off of you completely. Only when you understand and identify what triggered the depression will you understand how to get rid of it. When you know the cause, you will not just mask it with mood-altering medication. You will get free of it once and for all. It is not God's best for you to stay depressed.

In this teaching, I'm going to share several Scriptures that have really meant a lot to me. You may think, *Well, those are just Scriptures.* Actually, they are God's road maps to show you what He has planned for you. He's telling you that you don't have to live with depression's chains paralyzing you.

God tells us to fear no evil no matter what: *"Yea, though I walk through the valley of the shadow of death, I will fear no evil"* (Psalm 23:4). Even if you are walking through the valley of depression, He is there with you. Yes, you will have periods of despair, pain, and loss during your life, but *never* set up camp and stay there!

Many times, trauma itself will bring on depression. Trauma can come from a variety of areas, such as divorce, death, financial ruin, loss of a job or career, traumatic injury, or loss of bodily function. When trauma comes in, the body produces a stress hormone that attacks your immune system, your joy, and your life. The only way to kill those stress hormones is endorphins. It sounds like a big word, doesn't it?

ASK GOD FOR A SPIRIT OF JOY

Where do you find endorphins? One way to produce them is to experience laughter. Sometimes, I tell people this and they say, "I'm so depressed, how am I supposed to laugh?"

Well, put your hands on your belly and just say out loud, "Father, give me a spirit of joy. Father, in the name of Jesus, I command what the enemy has stolen to be restored. Right now, I want my joy and my life to be restored."

As this book continues, you are going to be saying a lot of prayers over different areas in your life. If that area really means a lot to you, I encourage you to come back to this chapter and pray that prayer again. Confess it and watch what God will do in your heart.

Write out some Scriptures or print them out—and not just the scriptural reference, but the whole verse. Once you write them down, I want you to say them out loud. Remember, *"faith comes by hearing, and hearing by the word of God"* (Romans 10:17). You need to start prophesying, speaking, and declaring these Scriptures over yourself:

For I know the thoughts that I think toward you, says the LORD, thoughts of peace and not of evil, to give you a future and a hope. Then you will call upon Me and go and pray to Me, and I will listen to you. And you will seek Me and find Me, when you search for Me with all your heart.
(Jeremiah 29:11–13)

Surely there is a future, and your hope will not be cut off.
(Proverbs 23:18 ESV)

Wait on the LORD; be of good courage, and He shall strengthen your heart. (Psalm 27:14)

DEPRESSION IS NOT PART OF GOD'S PLAN

God declared that He doesn't just have a plan for you, He has an *awesome* plan for your life. These words are meant to give you hope. Depression is definitely not part of a good and hopeful future.

What you are going through is temporary. It can become permanent, but you need to choose your future. Are you going to accept or reject that depression? I hope that after reading this chapter, you will listen to me and definitely reject it. Like King David, confidently declare to the Lord:

Even when I walk through the darkest valley, I will not be afraid, for you are close beside me. Your rod and your staff protect and comfort me.
(Psalm 23:4 NLT)

You have no reason to make camp, mourn, and grieve in your depression. You need to get up and get moving. Run through the valley of the shadow of death and come out on fire in Jesus's name.

This Scripture warns us that there will be opportunities to overcome. Many people will experience a valley experience during their journey. This does not mean that you are to just accept such pain and stay there. Trauma and grief sometimes give people an excuse to stagnate in their sorrow. I want to encourage you again. Don't stay there.

The eternal God is your refuge, and underneath are [His] everlasting arms; He will thrust out the enemy from before you, and will say, "Destroy!" (Deuteronomy 33:27)

This verse is referring to a place of rest for you, a place of comfort, peace, and protection. There is nothing like being in the arms of someone who loves you. Even though you may not have a physical person there to hug you, God desires to wrap His arms around you to protect, love, and embrace you.

> *Anxiety in a man's heart weighs him down, but a good word makes him glad.* (Proverbs 12:25 ESV)

If you know somebody who's depressed, share an encouraging word from your Father God.

One day, I was with a fifty-four-year-old gentleman who had beautiful blue eyes and a great smile. Because of his deformed body, I don't think anybody noticed his features or ever commented on his smile. I don't think he had ever received a compliment in his life.

When I told him about his great smile and beautiful eyes, he started laughing. He actually got a little embarrassed because he didn't know how to handle a compliment. But those few words did more for his immune system and his depression than anything else. When he left, he was laughing with pure joy. In my opinion, he will never ever be the same.

JESUS WANTS YOU TO BE FREE

After any emotional roller coaster experience, realize and focus on the fact that Jesus wants you completely free from fear, anxieties, and other emotional chains.

As I was flying into Houston one day, I looked out the window to admire God's wonderful creation. I saw many lakes and ponds down below, but I also saw an ugly green buildup of algae hiding their natural beauty. Where these bodies of water didn't have fresh water coming in, there was no stirring in the water. Their beauty was slowly and surely being covered by algae.

As I looked down, I thought, *That area used to be covered with beautiful lakes and ponds. But a little junk came in, followed by stagnation. Nothing fresh is coming in.*

God showed me a powerful analogy. If a beautiful Christian doesn't get fed, they change because the Word of God is not nourishing their soul. Fellowship with one another and encouraging words are absent. I realized people who are suffering from depression need more God to stay healthy and happy. His Word will get the murk, the muck, and the mire out of your life. That junk feeds depression.

PUT YOUR TRUST IN GOD

God wants to help you manage and control your emotions. He wants you to just trust Him with your emotions. He can and will release your depression.

Cast your burden on the LORD, and He shall sustain you; He shall never permit the righteous to be moved. (Psalm 55:22)

Our bodies are not meant to carry the weight of trauma or the heaviness of depression. Many times, people have experienced trauma and gotten depressed. Their shoulders droop, their back tends to bow over, and their head goes down. Very rarely do they walk with their head up and their eyes focused straight ahead into their future.

He sent from above, He took me, He drew me out of many waters. He delivered me from my strong enemy, from those who hated me. For they were too strong for me. They confronted me in the day of my calamity, but the LORD was my support. He also brought me out into a broad place; He delivered me because He delighted in me. The LORD rewarded me according to my righteousness; according to the cleanness of my hands He has recompensed me. For I have kept the ways of the LORD.

(2 Samuel 22:17–22)

When I read, "*I have kept the ways of the LORD,*" I am reminded of Job, who lost everything. He had the opportunity to get depressed. Even though the word *depressed* isn't in the book of Job, I'm sure he got both depressed and discouraged. His wife said, "*Curse God and die*" (Job 2:9). But Job didn't listen to her. And in return, the Word says in Job 42 that Job received twice as much as he had before. Here's the key: when he started praying for his friends, he moved from his saddened condition and reached out to others who he probably thought were in a worse condition.

DEPRESSION CAN BLIND US

A depressed person has little joy for life. In my opinion, it's a sadness that has taken root and turned into hopelessness and worthlessness. We need to use our spiritual eyes to see through these murky times. Often, a person is blinded by depression. Don't let strong emotions and emotional turmoil take your identity away. It's very important that you not allow depression to become your identity. By this, I mean people may identify you as the person who's "always depressed."

> And the ransomed of the LORD shall return, and come to Zion with sing-
> ing, with everlasting joy on their heads. They shall obtain joy and gladness,
> and sorrow and sighing shall flee away.   (Isaiah 35:10)

It's very important to understand and be able to recognize symptoms of depression. In addition to those I mentioned at the beginning of this chapter, symptoms can include a lack of concentration, fatigue, erratic emotions, sleep issues (too much or too little), unexplained aches and pains, weight gain or inability to maintain weight, anxiety, social withdrawal, general unhappiness, and irritability.

TYPES OF DEPRESSION

PTSD-Related

Research suggests that those with PTSD are more likely to experience depression and people who are depressed are more likely to experience anxiety or stress. People who've had PTSD at some point in their lives are three to five times more likely to develop depression than individuals who didn't experience PTSD.

Both depression and PTSD can affect your mood, interests, energy levels, and emotions. Symptoms for both can include trouble sleeping or sleeping too much; emotional outbursts, including anger or aggression; and loss of interest in activities.

People with PTSD may have greater anxiety around specific people, places, or things as a result of a certain traumatic event, but depression often occurs and worsens independent of any life event.

Seasonal Affective Disorder

Seasonal affective disorder (SAD) is a type of emotional depression that occurs during certain times of the year, particularly during the winter months. It is more common in women than in men.

Alaskans may have a more severe problem with SAD than Americans in the Lower Forty-eight because our northernmost state receives very few hours of sunlight during the winter months. People in Seattle, Washington, may also experience SAD because their region receives so much rain and limited sunshine. Additionally, people work inside year-round and don't spend a lot of time outside when they are not working can also suffer from SAD.

Symptoms of this depression are more frequent and often difficult to control. Steps should be taken to prevent SAD because it can open the door for major depression.

Blood test results on those with SAD often reveal a vitamin D deficiency. Vitamin D is absorbed into the human body from sunshine. Taking a nice walk outside occasionally during daylight hours is usually all that is needed to give your body a boost of vitamin D. In some cases, special indoor lights may be used to help those with SAD.

Bipolar

Bipolar disorder is a condition in which people experience drastic mood swings, from feeling very happy, overconfident, and impulsive to feeling depressed, tired, and irritable. This condition can often be controlled with medication and counseling.

Postpartum

Many new mothers can feel depressed after their baby is born. Postpartum depression may be caused by hormonal changes or fluctuations, feelings of inadequacy or doubt in caring for a newborn, a history of depression, fatigue, lifestyle changes, and other factors.

DEPRESSION MAY WORSEN

Sometimes, symptoms of depression can exacerbate or get worse, especially if the person is holding on to a victim mentality. Accepting that this is as good as it gets, forgetting the joy of your salvation, or claiming the condition as your own will hinder your healing.

Psalm 51:12 (ESV) says, "*Restore to me the joy of your salvation, and uphold me with a willing spirit.*" Don't accept defeat, hopelessness, or a lack of self-worth.

> The LORD also will be a refuge for the oppressed, a refuge in times of trouble. And those who know Your name will put their trust in You; for You, LORD, have not forsaken those who seek You.   (Psalm 9:9–10)

God will not forsake you when you seek Him. He is telling you what to do if you are oppressed or in trouble.

TAKE HEART AND WAIT FOR THE LORD

Psalm 27:14 (ESV) says, *"Wait for the LORD; be strong, and let your heart take courage; wait for the LORD!"* This verse doesn't mean you should just sit down, stay depressed, and wait. It means you should serve the Lord while He works things out for your good.

If you feel depressed, start giving to others. That doesn't mean handing out all of your money. It means you should give them your time and attention.

Go to a nursing home and ask, "Who hasn't had a visitor in a long time?" Take them a flower or a book. Share a hug. Just talk and listen to them. Often, these people are more lonesome and depressed than you are. You'll receive so much more in return just by sharing the love of Jesus with them. I encourage you to find someone who just needs to talk and be there for them.

DON'T OPEN DOOR TO DEPRESSION

Many things can trigger depression, including trauma, grief, fear, and music. Yes, music. Obviously, I do not mean praise and worship music. Pay attention to the lyrics of a song, not just the melody. I heard a song the other day and its basic message was, "I'm going back to bed because I'm going to have a depressing day."

My first thought was that when this song is played, people are going to sing it. They don't realize what they're singing. Be careful what you listen to.

Pay attention to the movies, TV shows, and online videos that you see. If the message is depressing, stay away or turn it off. Do you feel as if you are experiencing what the characters are actually facing? This can open up the door for depression and stress. Sing, listen to, and watch happy things!

Withdrawing from friends and family who have hurt you, the death of a close friend or a loved one, divorce, loss of a job, continual financial struggle, and overwhelming debt can all lead to depression. What you do next is the key to fighting it.

To everything there is a season, a time for every purpose under heaven: a time to be born, and a time to die; a time to plant, and a time to pluck what is planted; a time to kill, and a time to heal; a time to break down, and a time to build up; a time to weep, and a time to laugh; a time to mourn, and a time to dance; a time to cast away stones, and a time to gather stones; a time to embrace, and a time to refrain from embracing; a time to gain, and a time to lose; a time to keep, and a time to throw away; a time to tear, and a time to sew; a time to keep silence, and a time to speak; a time to love, and a time to hate; a time of war, and a time of peace. (Ecclesiastes 3:1–8)

That is one of my favorite Scriptures because it explains that every aspect of life comes and goes. Signs of depression may come, but they also have to leave. Amen?

READ GOD'S WORD OFTEN

It's important to line up your thoughts and words with the Word of God. You need to read the Word often; I recommend reading it out loud. All versions of the Bible are available on CDs, DVDs, and smart phones. You can listen to it in the car or play it on your TV with fabulous scenery behind it. Plug in your earphones and listen to it twenty-four hours a day, whether you feel like reading it or not. God's Word is available.

Prophesy His Word daily. Speak to the dry and thirsty areas of your life. Listening to praise and worship does so much to fill your heart and soul. Plug in a soaking CD and just bask in His presence. You don't have to do anything except lie there and allow His presence roll over you.

You need to see yourself the way God intended and not the way people look at you. Ask Him for the fastest plan and the quickest route to get out of depression.

The LORD is near to the brokenhearted and saves the crushed in spirit. Many are the afflictions of the righteous, but the LORD delivers him out of them all. (Psalm 34:18–19 ESV)

The Lord delivers us from *all* of our troubles. He never leaves you and He doesn't forsake you. He will not leave you in the valley when you're broken and sad, beat down, and unsuccessful. Why would He leave you in the valley? Why would He even leave you at all? If you find yourself in the valley, you need to really draw closer to God. God doesn't like to see you in the valley; He's there with you to encourage you to climb out. One step at a time, climb to the mountaintop of victory.

The steps of a man are established by the LORD, when he delights in his way; though he fall, he shall not be cast headlong, for the LORD upholds his hand. (Psalm 37:23–24 ESV)

Even when you trip and stumble, the Lord holds your hand. It's okay to be upset; these things happen. Getting angry is okay, too. Just don't let that anger grow into bitterness because it will also play emotional havoc on you. Learn to maintain an emotional balance.

> *Why are you cast down, O my soul? And why are you disquieted within me? Hope in God; for I shall yet praise Him, the help of my countenance and my God.*
>
> (Psalm 43:5)

Look in your Bible and consider King David, who grieved over his son's death. He felt like he was a failure where God was concerned. I believe many of the psalms portray his heart crying out to God from a state of depression. He needed and wanted God's help.

> *Answer me speedily, O Lord; my spirit fails! Do not hide Your face from me, lest I be like those who go down into the pit. Cause me to hear Your lovingkindness in the morning, for in You do I trust; cause me to know the way in which I should walk, for I lift up my soul to You.*
>
> (Psalm 143:7–8)

AVOID DEPRESSION

Here are some ideas on how to avoid depression using natural means:

+ Find an accountability partner or a mentor. If you've battled with depression in the past or are going through it right now, find that person you can openly talk to and pray with. An accountability partner can help you regain focus on your life and set realistic goals and priorities.

+ Identify expectations that are not being met by yourself or others. Are your expectations realistic or possible?

+ Do not mentally replay traumatic situations or arguments. You can have an argument with your parents, spouse, or someone else, or stew over an event, and play it again and again, over and over, in your head. Change your focus.

+ Get the right amount of sleep for your body. Avoid oversleeping or not sleeping enough. Create a better focus to achieve better health.

+ Get some exercise. It doesn't have to be strenuous. Take a nice walk outside and enjoy God's sunshine. If it's rainy or gloomy, walk in an enclosed mall.

+ Join activities that interest you that will boost your self-esteem and self-image. Get a haircut or try a new style, get a facial or manicure, visit a massage therapist, take a class in something that interests you like cooking, woodworking, photography, or art, or start a garden. Reconnect with friends.

+ Don't mask the symptoms of depression with alcohol or drugs. Those symptoms may seem to disappear, but they return with a vengeance as soon as the effects of the alcohol or drugs wear off. If you are on any form of antidepressants from a doctor, do not stop them without consulting your physician, who can verify your healing and give you further instructions.

+ Focus on giving time and helping others, like visiting a nursing home. Find an area to serve others, whether at a hospital, church, school, or some nonprofit organization. Volunteer for a cause that's important to you.

You keep him in perfect peace whose mind is stayed on you, because he trusts in you. Trust in the LORD forever, for the LORD GOD is an everlasting rock. (Isaiah 26:3–4 ESV)

This is a very important Scripture that I love. We can pray with confidence, "Father, keep my mind in perfect peace. Keep my heart in perfect peace because my mind is steadfast on You. In Jesus's name, amen."

We're going to pray some more in just a few moments and I believe in the name of Jesus that you're going to be completely set free of the spirit of depression.

DELIVERED FROM SCHIZOPHRENIA

I prayed for someone the other day who has schizophrenia, which often leads to depression. He was so excited, he just wanted to go off his medication immediately. His sister brought him to see me after he had seen his doctor. He actually looked different, acted different, and sounded different after I prayed for him. It was awesome. I talked to his sister and to him.

"You make sure you listen to your sister," I told him. "She's going to watch your emotional state to make sure you completely walk out your healing." I told his sister, "Keep an eye on him. Make sure that he walks out his healing completely."

At last report, he was doing great.

Fifty percent of people who have been severely depressed will fall back into depression, but that is *not* going to happen to you. Be aware and make sure you have an accountability partner to keep an eye on you and pray with you in the event that symptoms ever try to sneak in again. Examine what brought it on. Avoid any kind of recurrence.

Read this Scripture often:

The Spirit of the Lord God is upon me, because the Lord has anointed me to bring good news to the poor; he has sent me to bind up the broken-hearted, to proclaim liberty to the captives, and the opening of the prison to those who are bound; to proclaim the year of the Lord's favor, and the day of vengeance of our God; to comfort all who mourn; to grant to those who mourn in Zion—to give them a beautiful headdress instead of ashes, the oil of gladness instead of mourning, the garment of praise instead of a faint spirit; that they may be called oaks of righteousness, the planting of the Lord, that he may be glorified. (Isaiah 61:1–3 esv)

First, understand that He wants to set you free from all of this. Second, He also wants to use you to set other people free of depression.

Supernatural therapies and prayer for the different areas of depression are most effective. I want to encourage you to place your hand on your heart, your head, and sometimes your belly—wherever you feel led with each prayer.

ELECTRICAL AND MAGNETIC FREQUENCIES

Part of the prayer is going to be for electrical and magnetic frequencies and chemicals to be in perfect harmony and balance. Any traumatic experience has an effect on your emotions and chemicals in your body. Two of those important chemicals are serotonin, which makes you happier, and melatonin, which helps you sleep. Doctors may offer you medications containing these chemicals or designed to make your body produce them to balance your emotions. Since your body can produce these chemicals on its own, why not just pray for chemicals in your body to be restored to normal?

You are going to pray for your body to produce and maintain healthy levels of chemicals in Jesus's name. This will also include endorphins, which reduce pain and boost pleasure, resulting in a feeling of well-being. You will also rebuke all of those stress hormones.

SOME PRAYERS FROM THE HEART

Keep in mind that you never have to say any of these prayers exactly as they are written. Pray the meaning of each prayer from your heart. For optimum effectiveness, say them out loud:

DEPRESSION

Father, in the name of Jesus, I curse the spirit of trauma and fear that has opened up the door to any kind of depression and oppression. I cut off any words from friends or family members and the medical field that say I am always depressed. I cut those words off in Jesus's name. Father, I thank You that today is a brand new day. My joy is coming back in Jesus's name.

Father, Your joy is coming on me today in Jesus's name. I curse any form of hopelessness, worthlessness, rejection, abandonment, anxiety, and feelings of loneliness. I speak life, health, and wholeness, into my mind, my body, and my soul right now in Jesus's name. I speak to my chemical and electrical frequencies to go back into perfect harmony and balance in Jesus's name. I command the melatonin and serotonin to rise up in my body to the proper amounts in Jesus's name. Father, replace all stress hormones with healthy endorphins in Jesus's name.

Father, I thank You for giving me greater clarity and direction in what you have called me to do in Jesus's name. I speak greater discernment and a greater sense of passion in protecting my heart and mind against the lies of the enemy. Father, I thank You that You have restored my vision in the natural as well as in the supernatural in Jesus's name. I curse any form of habit, dependency, or label of being "depressed" in Jesus's name.

Father, I thank You for speaking to my heart right now and that any hindrance to hearing Your voice and direction for my life will be completely destroyed in Jesus's name. I choose life with total freedom from depression in Jesus's name. I am making a commitment to draw near to You, Lord, like never before. I desire to communicate with You in prayer, in Your Word, and around other Christians. I now know and understand I can resist the lies of the enemy that are coming against me, and I can fight back and be victorious in every way. In Jesus's name. Amen.

FINANCES

Other areas of life can also bring on depression. One of those is financial problems. This is very important to get rid of the depression brought on from financial problems. The Lord says He will supply all of your needs according to His riches and glory. (See Philippians 4:19.) Psalm 37:4 (ESV) says, "*Delight yourself in the LORD, and he will give you the desires of your heart.*"

God does not lie. He tells you in His Word that He wants to give you more than your needs. He wants to bless you and He wants to give you joy. All He asks is your obedience to His Word. Simply said, obedience brings His blessings. Some people don't tithe; they're not giving offerings and they are not giving their time. Ignoring God is disobedience. Just repeat these prayers aloud:

Father, I repent for not giving of my tithes and offerings as You have directed. I ask You to put those sins on the cross of Jesus Christ and cover them with His blood. I now commit all I possess and earn to You. I affirm my complete dependency on You for all I need. I renew my covenant relationship with You financially, and will freely and joyfully give You my tithes and offerings in Jesus's name.

Father, I thank You right now in the name of Jesus that You are blessing those who I give to and that You're giving me good soil to plant my seed. Father, I thank You for multiplying back what I give like You promise in Deuteronomy 1:11. I thank You that my debts are being supernaturally cancelled and overall debt reduction is happening very quickly. Father, I release my finances to You. I curse the spirit of poverty and the poverty mindset that I have carried in the past. Father, I thank You that You're going to rain down supernatural provision for me and my family in Jesus's name. Amen.

LONELINESS

Depression can be brought on by loneliness. Jesus promised that He would never forsake you or leave you. He will always be with you. (See Hebrews 13:5 and Romans 8:38–39.) He surrounds you with protection of His angels. (See Psalm 91:11 and Luke 4:10.)

Father, thank You that You are surrounding me with angels. You are surrounding me with Your love and Your Holy Spirit to comfort me and lead me. Give me a heart for others. Draw me into a relationship with those whom I can walk with in Your Spirit. Give me new relationships with those who love You so that I can love them and also be loved in return. Thank You, most of all, for being the Lover of my soul, the Light of my eyes, the Lifter of my soul. Your love for me never falters or fails. Thank You for all Your blessings. In Jesus's name. Amen.

DEATH OF A LOVED ONE

You may be depressed due to the death of a spouse, friend, parents, or another loved one. Read some comforting Scriptures (see Psalm 118:14; Habakkuk 3:19; 2 Corinthians 12:9) and say this prayer aloud:

Thank You, Lord Jesus, for the time that I had with my mom, my dad, other family members, and friends. Thank You for all the good experiences we had together. Thank You that all relationships in You are eternal and that I will see them again. I know I cannot live the rest of my life under a cloud of grief. I curse the spirit of trauma and grief and command it to leave because it's trespassing on God's property. I command it to leave now, in Jesus's name. Thank You, Jesus. And I thank You that You are my strength, and that I can live happily in You. In Jesus's name. Amen.

(More prayers are offered in chapter eighteen.)

My mom, Frances Hunter, died a few years ago. It was expected because she was ninety-three years old and her health was failing. When her earthly body died, there was a spirit of grief and trauma that came on me. It affected my voice and ministry. I recognized what it was because I had prayed with other people with the same problem.

I hardly had a voice, but I said, "Father, right now, I curse the spirit of trauma and grief that's trying to come in and destroy me. I command it to go in Jesus's name. I command my voice to come back, in Jesus's name."

I ended with a loud, "Hallelujah!" I looked around to see if my mom was there because it sounded just like my mom. I was healed and free!

You have a choice to live in depression or not. You have a choice to take on the trauma victim mentality. You have a choice to live in that grief or not. I've missed my mom and dad many times and in many ways, but I'm no longer grieving for them. That spirit left instantly because I did not want to keep it. I did not want it to prevent me from talking to you today. I am praying for you:

> Father, right now in the name of Jesus, I speak a blessing over all those who are reading this book and listening to You in their spirit. Father, in Jesus's name, I speak life, health, wholeness, blessings, financial breakthrough, an increase in endorphins, serotonin level, and all of the above. Father, I praise You for what You have done in this life this day. In Jesus's name, amen.

★ 5 ★

BROKEN-HEART SYNDROME

We all have heard people talking about having a broken heart. When people who have been married for a long time die within a few days of each other, it's often blamed on broken-heart syndrome. This condition is real and can be triggered by very stressful situations, like the death of someone you love, a break-up, or another high-stress situation, even a surprise party or winning the lottery.

This syndrome may cause acute heart failure, lethal heart irregularities, and ventricular rupture. Broken-heart syndrome is also known as stress-induced cardiomyopathy. There is a sudden temporary weakening of the muscle of the heart, which can cause symptoms similar to a heart attack. The symptoms of broken-heart syndrome are treatable if caught early enough and the condition usually reverses itself in about a week.

A TESTIMONY ON
BROKEN-HEART SYNDROME

Just read your posting on "Broken-Heart Syndrome." It is *absolutely* a real thing.

I was taken by ambulance to the hospital in November 2018 with severe abnormal heart rhythms. No heart attack. No pain. My heart simply would not function normally. After many weeks of tests, a few medications, and wearing a heart monitor, a cardiologist diagnosed my *condition* as broken-heart syndrome. I drove and met you at a meeting in Colorado, where you prayed for me on December 6, 2018—my sixtieth birthday.

Today my heart is working "normally." I am still taking one medication, a mild one for blood pressure, which may no longer be necessary once I lose weight.

What happened? I had experienced loss, stress, and was dealing with grief, regrets, and disappointments. It all *literally broke my heart.*

It was a lesson learned by almost dying. The answer is to *give it all to Jesus*. Hold nothing in too long…it will eat you up from the inside out.

I have made life changes and intentionally strive to embrace life and *joy*.

Your prayers and kindness toward me were a blessing from God on that day. I pulled myself together, learned to breathe again—and to *live*.

Much love, honor, and respect. BRD

★ 6 ★

ADDICTION

How does it start? Often, it starts slowly, but surely. A friend offers a cigarette. You don't really like the smell, but all the cool people around seem to hang together with a cigarette in their fingers as they share their stories and tales. You want to be cool and accepted, so you inhale that first puff and fight the urge to cough. Pretty soon, you are inviting others to share a cigarette and join the *macho* groups of friends or buddies.

One day, someone invites you to share a joint of marijuana. That is just a fancy cigarette, right? Wrong!

The subtle effects of getting "high" from marijuana relieves your stress and you continue lighting up, another and another, more frequently...until you don't want to be without it.

Next, comes the opiates, the drugs sold in the dark alleys. Maybe it's a prescription drug, legal or illegally obtained, that helps to relieve the pain. Of course, your decision-making ability flies out the window, along with your job. If you have a family, they fade into the distance if they remain at all.

Whether the first cigarette, a joint or an opiate, you usually need a drink to be included in your new group of friends, so have a swig of alcohol to add to the rush. Have another and another. It won't take long before you need the drugs to cover your pain, relieve your stress, and dream in whatever corner you have chosen to hide in.

Soon, more drugs like heroin, codeine, and other "new" things that are the latest craze find their way into your self-destruction.

Instead of easing your pain, you have chosen to magnify it. Instead of one or two sources of stress, you have the devil's lies coming from every direction. The things you valued are disappearing: your family, your occupation, your true friends...and God. Soon afterward, you recognize and acknowledge the slippery slope of destruction you have fallen into, and the lie of suicide enters in.

The latest statistics I found stated that there are twenty-two veterans committing suicide in the United States *every day*. What a loss! Brave men and women who served faithfully can't find the answer leading back to normal, productive lives.

Ministering to so many of these men and women is what triggered my desire to write this book. There are many testimonies throughout these pages from those I have met. I simply ministered God's Word and His healing to them. All I requested was a note to let me know what happened to them after they got healed.

Wow! I have gotten so many testimonies by mail and phone calls into the Joan Hunter Ministries offices. God gave me the heart to share His Word. He showed me the revelation of healing of memories, stress, and trauma. He healed me! Now, I can share that healing with others. Many of the healed veterans are now sharing their healing and ministering to others.

God is so good!

★ 7 ★

A DEATH WISH

When I was first diagnosed with breast cancer in 2000, I was lying on the exam table looking at the sonogram and saw how bad it looked. My first thought was excitement, *This is awesome! I can die and be with Jesus! I won't hurt anymore.*

If you don't understand that kind of pain, thank God!

There was such an aching in my heart, you can't fathom the pain. Death was the only option I thought I had to get rid of the horrendous pain. Suddenly, however, I determined that I had four excellent reasons to survive and not die: my four daughters.

As I laid on that cold table, I declared, "I will live and not die! I will proclaim the works of the Lord!"

As I minister around the world, I have prayed for many people who don't believe they can make it one more day. They have a variety of reasons for wanting to give up and die. Many people are hurting because their spouse or child died. Maybe a friend died in place of you in a dangerous accident or act of war. Occasionally, a person has made a death covenant such as, "I can't live without them!" A death covenant is often followed by physical ailments and allows the spirit of suicide to enter.

THE ENEMY IS LYING

The enemy's goal is to destroy you. He may sit on your shoulder and whisper in your ear. After hearing his lies, you may begin to believe what he says.

A death wish sounds like this: "Father, just take me home. My family will be much better off if I am gone. I wish I was dead! I am such a burden!"

If you give in to this evil spirit and commit suicide, you will spread that hurt and pain to your family and friends. Nothing is solved. The pain has simply multiplied.

You can break this covenant in Jesus's name. Read Jeremiah 29:11: *"For I know the thoughts that I think toward you, says the LORD, thoughts of peace and not of evil, to give you a future and a hope."*

In fact, read this verse many times. Print it out and post it on your mirror, your refrigerator, and your computer. Read it out loud every day!

Right now, repeat this prayer:

Father, I command this assignment of death to go from me in Jesus's name. I will live and declare the works of the Lord. The enemy wants to destroy me, but I seek life. I will serve You, Father!

You may need to read Jeremiah 29:11 and pray this prayer frequently at first. Get the words down deep in your soul. Chase the enemy out of your life, your home, and your mind. Welcome God's Word, His Son, and His Spirit to clean out all the hidden areas of your life and fill you up with Him.

He will give you peace and fill you with His love. He has special plans for you.

A TESTIMONY ON SUICIDAL THOUGHTS

I was fourteen. It was three o'clock in the morning. I lay there miserable, aching in pain that felt as physical as it was emotional. My head ached and my face was hot from all my tears that had poured from my eyes for the last several hours. I was spent. I could see nothing changing. I was afraid. I was angry. I was tired of hurting and acting like I was fine.

Nobody knew the torment in my mind from the years of keeping secrets. Not even anyone in the house knew. I was very good at playing the part. I looked like the best-behaved teenager any parent could have. I was active at my church in the youth group and helping in children's church. I had almost straight A's if you didn't count math.

Every parent-teacher conference was the same, "She is a joy to have in class. We wish we had more like her." From the outside looking in, it was a perfect kind of life. It was this masquerade that I was so exhausted from hiding behind. Now the place I didn't always have to be on guard was in its own state of turmoil.

I told the Lord I just wanted it all to end. I was tired. I would rather be with Him. I thought over the plan that had been forming. I knew where my father's gun cabinet was. I had shot some of those weapons before. I knew where the key was and I knew the right way it needed to be done. Without hesitation, I knew what I was going to do.

The Lord Speaks

The minute my feet hit the ground, I heard the Lord speak to me in a loud audible voice from over my shoulder, *"What do you think you're doing?"* It was firm and loud yet soft and gentle. I felt not only disapproval, but pain that I was causing His heart, all in one moment. I crumpled to my knees on the floor beside my bed with my face buried in my blankets to silence my sobs. I was crying out like I never had before.

All of the realization of what the ramifications of my action would have caused, not only to my family but to the heart of God, hit me like a ton of bricks. When I had words, these were the ones I spoke: "Lord, You have to change things, or next time, I will do it."

Within the next thirty days, my life was completely changed and the safe haven that was my home returned. Even if the secrets remained, at least the turmoil in my house had abated and I knew there was at least one realm of my world where God had moved mountains.

I needed to know Him more. I began to talk with Him like I hadn't before. I wanted to *know Him*, not just know *about* Him.

Through the next several years, I wish I could say I never had thoughts of taking my life again, but I did. The difference now was that I didn't want to disappoint God. I had to figure a way around the pain and torment that no one knew about. I felt like a failure for not being strong enough, not being good enough.

Self-Injuring Begins

Thoughts that a good daughter would not keep such horrible secrets only fed the vicious cycle of thinking, *I must be a disappointment, I am a horrible daughter*, and *I deserve to be punished*. Those thoughts led to self-injuring. I figured this was not suicide and therefore self-inflicted bruises and sometimes cuts were an acceptable option.

This behavior was also done in secret and I was careful enough to not leave bruises where anyone could see them. Usually my abdomen, hips, upper legs, and sometimes lower legs were the places I would beat over and over with a hairbrush or a stick of some sort. The wave of turmoil would lessen as a bruise would deepen. The physical pain would actually decrease as the emotional pain would decrease.

This release worked for several years until I was unable to keep the bruises hidden from my spouse. He got so angry. His words were the Lord in my ear: "How dare you do that to MY body. When we married, we became one flesh, so you are beating my body." And then he left and I didn't know if he was coming back or not. When he did, we began to talk about the things going on in my head and the lies I believed at the time.

The self-injuring ceased, but the desire was still there at times, as were the whispered thoughts of, *Wouldn't it just be easier if...* After the death of our first child, there was a very dark period of depression. I thought about suicide almost daily for a while. I knew that it wasn't the right answer and I begged God to take the thoughts away. In so many areas, God was proving Himself on my behalf, but the thought would still come. It was a constant fight and then it would be gone for days, weeks, or even years, only to resurface as if it had been lying dormant.

Learning from Joan Hunter

In the last four years, I have come to meet and study the teachings of Joan Hunter. Listening to her teachings on trauma and cellular memory have changed my life. There has been healing in my heart and life like I never knew were possible. I am completely different since being introduced to Joan Hunter Ministries. God has healed those areas that used to torment me. I have grown spiritually, understanding more about spiritual warfare and a very real spiritual enemy.

I have learned about cutting off generational curses and closing the doors in my soul that left me open to spiritual attacks. I have come to understand that wounds of my soul allowed the enemy to torment me. I learned the importance of taking back the authority that is mine when fighting the enemy of my soul. God gives me tools. God strengthens me and as I overcome, I take back dominion and territory that are rightfully mine.

In February 2019, my husband had a business trip for five days. The Lord and I had some hard conversations after the children were in bed a few of those nights. One night, as I was telling the Lord how hard this battle was, I was walking around my room. At that moment, I was doing more complaining—"Lord, this is hard, I don't know if I can do it"—than I was claiming, "Lord, with You, I can do this."

The Handgun and the Devil

As I was walking, my back had a crazy bad itch, so I opened my husband's bedside table to use his amazing back scratcher. Also in that drawer, just for the week he was gone, my husband had left his handgun for me. I have taken a gun safety course with him and actually have a concealed carry permit, so it is not unusual to have the handgun close and not at all frightening for me.

However, in that moment, I heard another voice in my room whispering in my ear: "It would be so easy. Your problems could be over in an instant. You would have such sweet relief." And as the words were being spoken, even though I was only staring at the gun and not touching it, I could feel the weight of it in my hand and the cold metal muzzle of it pressed to my face.

I became instantly angry. How dare the devil try talking to me like that! I was so angry that I threw the back scratcher in the drawer and slammed it shut so hard that it tipped the lamp. I started whisper-yelling so I wouldn't wake the kids, but I pointed my finger and laid into the evil spirit I now knew was behind this moment.

"God Reigns Here"

"You get out of here—I don't listen to you anymore," I declared. "You have no right to be here. This is *my* house and *God* reigns here. You are trespassing and a *liar*! You have no right to speak to me anymore. You get out of here in the name of Jesus!"

I had my finger pointed as I physically walked and shouted at it until I got to the front door. I opened that door and, in my mind, ushered it out of my house, giving it the what-for the whole time. Shaking my finger and stomping my foot, I yelled, "And don't you dare come back here, ever!" Then I slammed the door shut and went into prayer in the spirit.

The next day, the encounter was lingering in my mind. I was a bit disturbed that it had happened and was questioning the Lord. I questioned why this had occurred after so many years. The Lord reminded me of that night when I was fourteen and thought about suicide. I was embarrassed by the mere thought of that fateful night.

God gently said, "*You cried out to Me that night and I fought for you. Last night, you fought for yourself!*" I realized God had allowed this fight with the enemy so that I could take dominion in this area.

Today, I know that with God, I can fight the enemies that He calls me to fight. I am called to help set others free from bondages that I remember so well. He delivered me and now calls me to be a deliverer of others.

Suicide is a battle in the mind that the enemy likes to keep secret. It is also one he likes to reuse. I had heard so many times of my mom's struggle with suicidal thoughts. I am convinced that demon hung around because he couldn't get her. Instead, he has tried to get me. Well, he has been served an eviction notice! Bless the Lord!

—B.J.L.

PART 2:
TESTIMONIES

8

KELLY "KELL" BALES

Complex Post-Traumatic Stress Disorder (C-PTSD)

As of the publication date of this book, I have spent over half of my life in the United States Air Force. It was a true honor to serve our nation as an Airman and reach the top 2 percent tier of the enlisted force upon retirement after twenty-three years. My Air Force journey started after attending three years at an incredible and prestigious college in Wisconsin. As awesome as my experiences were, at the time, I just felt like I was on the wrong path inside. The Air Force provided an excellent opportunity to refocus and chart a new course. It was the best decision of my life, only to be trumped later in life by marriage to my incredible wife and the birth of our children.

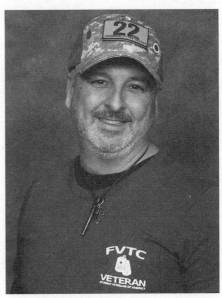

Kelly "Kell" Bales

Unlike most careers, when you're serving in the military, you are essentially *on call* 24/7/365. Additionally, you are held to a much higher standard—as it should be—in all areas of your life, including physical training, integrity, excellence, and work ethic, but also in personal areas like family and finances.

HIGH, SELF-IMPOSED STANDARDS

I know I often felt like I was walking on coals, constantly doing all I could to fulfill every requirement and meet every regulation 100 percent of the time.

Those self-imposed standards were very taxing on my body, mind, and spirit, especially as a perfectionist at the time. Although my typical work week was a fairly standard forty or forty-five hours, I had to be ready at the drop of a dime to deploy anywhere in the world. Again, that brought with it a whole new set of challenges, especially when I started a family.

Many of these issues, especially as I progressed up in rank, would weigh very heavy on me at times. Yet as a leader, I knew I had to lead by example, so I would often repress my own issues to help others with their life challenges. I could not imagine the amount of trauma on my body, slowly building up over the years, especially with such physical and mental demands. I am grateful for those leaders who were willing to help me through my issues when I'm sure they had their own as well. It was my wingmen, my accountability partners, who helped me through several difficult moments. As a wingman to others, my heart was to help them, too. It's just what we do.

I am proud to have served my nation as an Airman. However, it did come at a high cost: financial challenges, missed important events, long-distance relationships, family separation, and even negative effects on my health. I thank the Lord that He never left me nor forsook me, even through the trials and tribulations, many of which were caused by my own willful decisions. There were many sorrow-filled moments, including times of loneliness and rejection. I know many others who shared my sentiments. Nevertheless, I persevered. I kept up the good fight.

Isaiah 40:31 (NLT) has been a true inspirational Scripture for me for years: *"But those who trust in the LORD will find new strength. They will soar high on wings like eagles. They will run and not grow weary. They will walk and not faint."*

There are many I know who persevered, too. They were wonderful mentors and role models. They continued to encourage others in spite of their own challenges. They had grit; they had courage! As time progressed and I climbed the promotion ladder, I quickly became a mentor, leader, and coach to many around me, too.

SOME JUST GIVE UP

Sadly, we also saw others who, for one reason or another, just gave up. I experienced firsthand many of the challenges our Airmen faced; some pressed through while some made a permanent decision by taking their lives. Truly tragic. Suicide continues to be a highly debated subject in the military. In my personal opinion, few address the root issues and as great as many leaders' intentions are, programs continue to fall short of eliminating suicides in the military due to their surface-level approaches.

On top of the military lifestyle and all that brings with it, military members still have to deal with all of life's other situations. In spite of my best intentions to save my first marriage, it ended in a bitter divorce. It wasn't until years after the divorce that I realized there was a very controlling and narcissistic spirit involved during those fifteen-plus years.

I endured much. I mourned; I rejoiced. I cried; I laughed. I felt alone; I felt embraced. I won; I lost. I kept silent; I spoke out. I hated; I loved. These, along with a myriad of other life events, were slices of my life over more than twenty-three years of service to our nation. I am a United States military veteran.

We are truly a unique breed. It has been said that when we joined the armed services, whether enlisted or officer, we wrote a check payable to Uncle Sam up to the ultimate price of our life. I praise the Lord that Uncle Sam never cashed my check, as much as I was willing to lay down my life for my fellow wingman. Sadly, we have lost too many men and women who did give the ultimate sacrifice.

John 15:13 (ESV) states, *"Greater love has no one than this, that someone lay down his life for his friends."*

The world of psychology would label me a victim of narcissistic abuse. They have even developed the term *narcissistic abuse syndrome.* If you dig even a little deeper, you will find the term *complex post-traumatic stress disorder* (C-PTSD), where the trauma is very similar to PTSD. As I studied this, I felt I definitely met all the criteria.

FINDING FREEDOM WITH JESUS

However, I have truly forgiven all involved, including myself. It was only through the power of the Holy Spirit and the Father's love expressed through His Son, Jesus Christ, that I went from victim to victor. Little by little, I walked out the freedom Jesus paid for on the cross of Calvary. I had to renew my mind daily (see Romans 12:2) to fully understand my identity and my authority in Christ.

After starting off well on my journey of healing after the divorce was final, the Lord knew I needed a strong partner to help me overcome the deep, hidden wounds from a lifetime of trauma. About a year later, He blessed me with an incredible, loving, caring, forgiving wife who truly personifies the virtuous wife found in Proverbs 31. She has selflessly sacrificed so much to help me on this journey.

Even as I transitioned from active duty to retirement, I could say she's been my *bobber* to keep my head afloat while Jesus is my anchor! Unfortunately, most veterans carry many challenges into their retirement years; I know I did. She has never left my side and has been with me through some of my darkest moments post-retirement. We thank the Lord that He has been our third strand and we started out honoring Him from the beginning. I can honestly say we are in an incredible place now and have overcome a lifetime of challenges in just a short five years. We both can only point back to the Lord for His grace and mercy.

ONE SUICIDE IS TOO MANY

As a retiree, we face new challenges through the transition all while carrying over many of our previous issues from our active service; this can really weigh heavily on a veteran and their family. Depending on the source, the statistics state approximately twenty-two veterans commit suicide every day. Some statistics include active duty, Guard, Reserves, and veterans in their calculations while others do not. Nonetheless, *one* veteran suicide is too many!

I honestly admit I have had very difficult times through the transition from active duty to retiree but I am finally finding my footing again. I understand the hopelessness, the feeling of *what now*, and having similar feelings of grieving, almost like a death of your career. Due to approximately a decade of phenomenal kingdom teachings, I have a deeply-rooted understanding of my identify in Christ. I cannot begin to fathom how difficult it must be for those who do not personally know Jesus. I decree shalom and love over them all.

I am extremely grateful to several individuals over the years who have sowed unconditional love and support through some of my darkest moments. The first person who walked with me through my difficult journey is Joyce Daniels. Not only did she share great kingdom insight, she was indirectly responsible for introducing me to a powerhouse couple, Marc and Kay Miller, who forever changed my life through their incredible Holy Spirit-filled life coaching program. I can proudly say I'm a licensed master life coach with their organization and consider them family.

THROW BLANKETS FOR VETERANS

The third most impactful individual is Joan Hunter. Through her healing school and ordination process, including all of the incredible resources, I learned a lot about myself and found deep healing in many areas of my life. I consider it an honor and privilege to call her a dear friend after several years of building our relationship. Additionally, there are a myriad of other individuals from whom I gleaned great insight, too. They are too numerous to mention here by name.

I'm very grateful to have teamed up with Joan Hunter Ministries to launch a Miracles Happen for Veterans throw blanket project. After dealing with my own struggles and seeing the often-hidden wounds of other veterans, I just knew an anointed blanket would bless countless others and I've already heard of several incredible testimonies by veterans, including healing from PTSD. Additionally, I continue to be an advocate for our veterans at every turn, focusing on faith-based approaches to bring comfort, healing, and love to veterans and their families.

I still have some physical ailments due to my years of service, but I'm slowly working through them as the Lord leads. I am so blessed to have met Joan Hunter and absorb an immense amount of love from her and her ministry. I have applied what I have learned through a myriad of resources and see healing result after result. I know that going through the healing school and ordination process, I learned a lot about myself and was truly set free in a plethora of areas, including breaking free of much trauma.

As my family continues on our journey, especially as forerunners, we pray the Lord leads us to love on countless others through their challenges and struggles, especially other military couples and veterans.

SHARE YOUR LOVE WITH A VETERAN

Before I finish, I have a simple request. When you see a veteran out and about or even in your own family, please shake their hand, give them a fist bump or a hug, or perhaps pay their meal bill; it will mean the world to them, even if not outwardly acknowledged. Many continue to carry deep wounds, most of which are not visible.

Veterans are a unique breed. We need your prayers and, most importantly, for each and every one of us to be the hands and feet of Jesus to those who were willing to lay down their life for you and me. God bless our veterans, God bless y'all, and God bless the USA.

—Kelly "Kell" Bales
USAF, Retired
Founder, FIREHub International's ENabled Veterans ministry

9

JESSE AND JESSIE HUDSON

Post-Traumatic Stress Disorder

Think about the Dr. Seuss book, *Oh, the Places You'll Go!* I'm fairly certain that you have heard these simple and yet profound words at some point in your lifetime. Dr. Seuss, Theodor Geisel, was known for his timeless childhood literature. However, his works display an obvious depth of both scholastic interest and an intimately defined spiritual wisdom.

My name is Jessie Hudson. I am a mother, a teacher, a daughter, and a friend. Along with those, I proudly hold the title of combat veteran's wife. I will never win the Nobel Peace Prize, become president of the USA, or win an Olympic gold medal. None of that is in the cards for me. I am an *average* middle-aged American woman who isn't always socially accepted or what society around us would call *normal*. I am different. I married a veteran! This is my testimony of hope and healing for veterans with post-traumatic stress disorder (PTSD).

My husband's name is Jesse Hudson. Yes, we have the same name. You can laugh—everyone else does.

MET IN COLLEGE

When I met Jesse, we were in college. We apparently had both signed up for Kinesiology 101. Jesse was in the Army and had been in for quite some time when we met. He'd already done a ten-month tour in Iraq as a gunner and combat convoy security driver. Please keep in mind this is my testimony, not his. I'm saying this because I love my husband and greatly respect him. I will not be telling his personal encounters and experiences while over in Iraq. This is being told to you by a combat veteran's wife's perspective of total healing, hope, and personal growth.

Our love grew deep and fast. To be totally honest, we moved along together much quicker than a normal Christian couple. But then again, we were anything but normal.

After Iraq, Jesse was angry and even unstable, to say the least. We fought more often than not and rarely agreed on anything. We both drank alcohol occasionally. Without going into a plethora of detail, alcohol led us to an abusive relationship.

Both of us were verbally abusive to one another and once or twice our battle was physical, causing me to fear him. I soon found myself out of church and living a life filled with chaos and depression. I came to an understanding that I had married my dad. I always told myself that I'd *never* do that.

EVERYONE SUFFERS

As the truth revealed itself over time, both of us learned that America's veterans, along with their spouses, their entire family, and even their pets, endure far too much and obtain very little added resources for success. I watched my family suffer, my husband suffer, and all anyone seemed to see was an unhappy and complaining wife.

So what is PTSD? Why do so many veterans feel hopeless, angry, and paranoid? I decided enough was enough. I always knew Jesus is Lord, but could He really be our Healer?

I thought, *Can Jesus take away all the trauma that both my husband and I endured as younger children? Can He heal me from wounds that cut so deep they are still closing up? Rape, molestation, abortion, and neglect…. How can God put a young man through so much and then send him off to war?*

I'm not going to lie; I do not know all the details about what went on over in Iraq. I *do* know the aftermath though: our own personal war zone, right in our own home. There were many times that the word *divorce* was thrown around. Our marriage just seemed hopeless and useless, like beating a dead horse. That's just something I do not want to do. After all, I'm a vegan.

During this time, we had gone back to church. As a wife and mother, I'd cry and weep out loud to my Father. I'd sing childhood psalms to renew my mind. I'd memorize Bible verses, write them on sticky notes, and post them all around my house. One of my favorites was Psalm 40:1: *"I waited patiently for the LORD; and He inclined to me, and heard my cry."*

DRAWN TO JOAN

I met Joan Hunter and something about her really resonated with my heart. It was such a pulling force that it almost physically drew me to her. Little did I know that she was about to preach to me on "hope of abundance."

She spoke words over my husband, who wasn't with me that night. She spoke healing over him and cursed trauma at its root. She had me repeat a few things and hugged me with a love that I never felt before. After the meeting, I spent the last of our money on a discounted blanket.

I was so desperate for the hope of healing over my husband, myself, and our whole family. It was time! I bought that blanket in faith and I didn't tell my husband about it. Instead, I washed our bedding and that night, I hid the blanket under our fitted sheet. As he slept on top of that anointed blanket, the healing started. From that day forward, each day, life changed for the better for my family.

Jesus can heal us but we need to *want* the Healer first. Not long after this, my husband was baptized at a revival and the chains broke off of him within moments. No more tobacco chewing, no more alcohol. He's healed and I am, too. I'm not saying life is sweet peaches and cream, but God did it! Miracles still happen!

THERE *IS* HOPE AND HEALING

Can I just speak straight to the veteran reading this for a few minutes? Life isn't always fun and it can get pretty ugly and dirty at times. But what you have done for America is by far the most grand of any gift that our nation and our people can possibly receive. If you feel hopeless, let me tell you that there *is* hope for the hopeless, rest for the weary, and love for your wounded soul.

If you are maimed, remember that your wife loves you very much. Even if the two of you fight, she's still by your side. She is wounded, too. You are both in this together. Jesus is your Hope and He is your Healer.

My husband and I do not have a perfect life. Jesus is still working on us. There is more healing to take place. Yes, we have grown leaps and seen an amazing amount of healings in our lives. Guess what? It is just the beginning. He has so much more for my husband, me, and our children.

When I look back, even just a year ago, I can see the work of His hands upon our lives. I wait with anticipation like a child who counts down the days before Christmas. I can't wait to see all He has for us a year from now—even two weeks from now.

DON'T LET PTSD WIN

PTSD can cripple those who serve, as well as their families. It silently creeps in behind the scenes. Don't lose your life or your family to PTSD. Find the support you are looking for. It is obvious that you are looking for support or you would not be reading this right now. There are people out there who want to help you, just like Joan Hunter.

You never expected to just welcome PTSD into your marriage or your life. Just like you would fight in combat, you must never stop fighting. PTSD is only one of the tactics of the enemy.

Keep going and keep pressing through. It is okay to have bad days, but those bad days do not define you. Your value and your worth are found in Jesus Christ. Remember, you are *never* alone. Abba Father is just waiting to listen to your cry. (See Psalms 40:1.) Miracles do still happen! I am a living witness to them. Healing *will* come. It may not come all at once. Sometimes, it is a process.

SPREAD BLESSINGS

A dear friend of mine, who is also my pastor, told me that every time I want to yell and scream or punch my veteran in the face, I should ask Father God to bless my husband instead. And as hard as it can be at times, I do it. That's not to say I don't call my pastor to vent every so often. I am busy in obedience and submission to Jesus. He takes me from glory to glory.

"Oh, the places you'll go." Suddenly, that is not just a saying from Dr. Seuss, but a prophetic word spoken over your life. Your healing is a journey of hope and love, redemption and freedom. Wait in expectation for your miracles to come…because they will.

Even in our pain, the King of all kings is working and fighting on your behalf. Whether you are the veteran or the spouse, let Him hide you in the shadow of His wings. (See Psalm 91:4.) The healing has already begun. It might be a bumpy ride at times, but keep your seatbelt fastened and wait to see all of the wonderful places you will go with Jesus, who will take you in the deep healing waters of His intimacy.

THE CRY OF A WARRIOR'S WIFE

Awake, my heart, to see who you are without the rifles and ammo. Make vivid my sight so I can see through your eyes as you watch the enemy sacrifice their own children. May my dreams come alive in the middle of the night, that I might be alert to your anxiously active mind. Will your paranoia ever leave or is it destined to be a hunting?

Will the doubt and the fears keep you out in our fields, looking for the Iraqis? I worry for you because I long to love you for all the days of my life. But you see, my dear husband, it is only so common that suicide secretly floods in, into the support groups of just us wives and the others who gather in prayer for the emotionally crippled and grieving.

PTSD—it is also killing me, our children, and the whole family. I understand, soldier husband, that yours is worse. That it is a curse so undeserving. At times, my heart roars and rages for the murders you have seen, along with plenty other gruesome things. PTSD, you don't care about him, our children, and certainly not me. *How dare you walk through our home as if it was your own, as if we were only visitors?*

UNBIDDEN VISIONS

Sometimes, when I see him wearing a shirt, blue jeans, and tie, I can't help but see his helmet. I see his rank and unit's name instead of the computer case. I see a hand holding a grenade instead of his Bible. I envision weapons, mental tactical lessons, and a rucksack full of ammo.

Husband, you are not alone. There *is* light ahead. I'll stand as your wife right by your side. I vowed to never leave you, in sickness or in health, for richer or poorer, even through this mental disorder called PTSD. When we cling to the cross because it is all that we've got, or as we soar on the clouds like we live above the sounds of the chaotic world, together forever we will be.

PTSD—get out of our way and be gone today! We don't accept you or want you. You are just a tool of destruction in the hands of the real enemy, Satan, who is as disgusting as you and used a radical group of Iraqis to hate, kill, and destroy.

Stand down while you can, PTSD. Make way for the King. Because one day soon, He is coming back to rule in powerful majesty. PTSD, you go to hell where you belong. When our Savior comes, your future will be never-ending, agonizing pain and heat.

But for my soldier and me, it will be an eternal symphony of joy and peace.

—Jesse Hudson, a combat veteran's wife,
a mother and a member of our PTSD family

★ 10 ★

SAMMY KEUHN

Vietnam Veteran and Police Officer with PTSD

As a teenager, Sammy Keuhn kept dreaming that he was in a war and someone was advancing to shoot him. He would wake every time...but the dream kept reoccurring, night after night. The dreams finally stopped right before the war broke out. He didn't have that specific dream again, but now, he was off to fight in a real war, not knowing if he would be shot and killed, or come home maimed.

As Sammy was leaving for war, his mother said something like, "God put you here for a reason." She gave him a little Bible to carry with him and made him say the sinner's prayer:

> Lord Jesus, I confess my sins and ask for Your forgiveness. Please come into my heart as my Lord and Savior. Take complete control of my life and help me to walk in Your footsteps daily by the power of the Holy Spirit. Thank You, Lord, for saving me and for answering my prayer. In Jesus's name. Amen.

Sammy said the prayer but did not realize what he was saying.

FLOWN INTO VIETNAM

Sammy was in a planeload of six hundred men flown into Vietnam at night. They had a three-minute window to disembark because the aircraft had to take off again. They were under fire the entire time, but were unarmed. Their weapons were waiting at their destination.

Six hundred men climbed into eight buses...but only the first three buses made it to base. The enemy destroyed five buses, killing everyone aboard. Riding in the third bus, Sammy got to the base shaken but safe.

He was among the first American troops in Cambodia and one of the last ones out. Fighting was like nothing he had imagined. Vietnamese soldiers would pop out of underground tunnels, do their damage, and then disappear again. God saved Sammy's life again and again, protecting him from harm.

LIVING THE NIGHTMARE

One day, out on the battlefield, he was struck by the realization that this was the place from his dreams years before. He saw the enemy fighter from his nightmare coming directly at him, ready to kill him. He pulled the trigger on his weapon—and nothing happened. It was jammed. As if God had somehow prepared him for what to do, Sammy tossed his weapon aside, grabbed his friend's gun, and shot the enemy dead. God had prepared him for that moment through his recurring nightmare. He just had to have the faith to trust God.

For a short time, the American public supported the war in Vietnam. President John F. Kennedy took a stand to support the government of South Vietnam and contain communism, just as President Dwight D. Eisenhower had done. The Vietnamese soldiers were armed by the Soviet Union and China. But by 1965, anti-war protests grew.

NO HERO'S WELCOME

Members of armed forces who came home from World War II were treated like the heroes they were, but those returning from Korea were ignored and those returning from Vietnam were often treated with scorn.

Sammy Keuhn

God protected Sammy from many enemy attacks; during one battle, three mortars exploded around him yet he was unharmed. Even so, he was wounded three times while serving in the Army. He eventually became a military advisor.

After returning home, Sammy suffered from sleep deprivation. When he did sleep, he had nightmares about battles he'd fought in the war.

Sammy became a police officer and suffered a leg injury in 1971 that required a metal rod implant. He developed blood poisoning and, to make matters worse, he was given the wrong blood type during a transfusion. Sammy had several silent heart attacks that dropped his heart function to 25 percent. This heart damage prevented any surgery when he went into liver failure and had a large stone in his gallbladder. He ended up with a pacemaker.

REFUSED TO ADMIT HE HAD PTSD

Sammy knew he was suffering from PTSD, but he felt that admitting this made a man look weak. This soldier-turned-policeman wouldn't seek help or even talk about his problems. While traveling, he had another heart attack, but refused to get treatment.

During his wife's ordination to ministry at one of Joan Hunter's conferences in 2015, Joan prayed for Sammy and the couple bought a "Miracles Happen! for Veterans" blanket.

Sammy's nightmares continued, but God spoke to him and he finally realized what was causing them. Sammy had kept photos of some of the enemy soldiers he had killed in the war. They were in his recurring dreams and he still felt hatred for them.

God said, "How long are you going to hold on to that hate? Burn it." He finally did burn those photos and the trauma went away. The nightmares ceased.

Sammy's heart function has improved to 45 percent and he ministers to veterans and others, praying for them wherever he goes. God is using him mightily with veterans and everyone else who just needs a touch from God.

★ 11 ★

CARMEN WILKINSON

Personal and Family History of PTSD; Disability

Military life in general can be traumatic in many ways, not only for the active duty members, but for their families—immediate, extended, and future generations. Trauma can occur during military service during times of war and peace. Whether caused by physical injury, post-traumatic stress disorder (PTSD) or both, the effects on a family can be devastating. No matter what generation or war, the world expects us to come back home and live a normal life like nothing ever happened. That's not only unrealistic, it's impossible in our own strength.

The world also says there's no cure for PTSD. We have to be medicated and learn how to *live with it*. My friends, I'm here to tell you there's no *coping* or true *living with* PTSD. Only God can heal the wounds of war and set us and our families free to truly live. I've experienced and made it through (praise Jesus!) both sides of PTSD as a family member of those with PTSD and as an Air Force veteran afflicted with it. There is hope and His name is Jesus.

WAR VETERANS ON ALL SIDES

I was born and raised in a military family. My grandfathers were both war veterans. My mom's father was a Marine in World War II. My dad's father was in the Air Force and served multiple tours in the Vietnam War. My dad was in the Air Force and I have many uncles who were in either in the Marines or the Air Force who also served in WWII, Vietnam, the Korean war, and much more.

After being raised in a military environment, being in the military myself was as natural as breathing. Not only was I accustomed to military life, I was very aware, at a young age, of the effects of war on a family. I didn't know what PTSD was as a child, but I knew my family members were suffering with tremendous pain that had something to do with what happened in war.

Even though I didn't understand it, I could see how their pain and the consequences of their actions negatively affected their entire families, myself included, in one way or another. I had no idea that one day I'd experience PTSD for myself and see it happen to my own family. Because of my experiences, I now understand what was really going on with my traumatized relatives and the effects that it's still having in their families.

MOM'S DAD LOST HIS LEG

Before I talk about what happened to me in the military, I'd like to tell you a little about my family when I was growing up. As a Marine in WWII, my mom's father not only lost a leg, he also had severe PTSD that led to alcoholism, family devastation, and death. My grandparents were very much in love and had eight kids. Grandma was and still is a mighty woman of God. No matter how much she loved him and tried to make it work, she couldn't help him. They got married and divorced twice. Grandpa was a loving man who'd give you the shirt off his back when he was sober, but anger and violence could easily take over when he drank...which was every day. So, you never knew which Grandpa you'd be dealing with. Grandma and her children had to work long hard hours to keep the family afloat.

I don't know everything that happened when my mom and her siblings were growing up, but as a child, I felt their pain and resentment toward him. I think they all had to grow up a lot faster than most. I watched my Grandpa go back and forth between having a job and a place to live to being homeless in his car drinking away his military pension. Oh, how he struggled. The whole family did. Some developed their own problems with addiction and anger. Instead of talking about things, everyone ignored or buried their problems.

I thank Jesus that He gave me the gift of compassion as a child. Even though I didn't understand it, I felt Grandpa's sadness and pain. I knew he didn't want to be an alcoholic or hurt anyone. He loved us all. He wouldn't talk about the war, but he did tell me he wished things were different. I loved on him no matter what and, thankfully, for whatever reason, he wasn't mean to me like he was to my cousins.

GAME TURNED VIOLENT

When I was ten years old, he was living in an in-law type of apartment we had on our property. He was trying to quit drinking. One day, I snuck into his place to grab his prosthetic leg and hide it. It was a game we played. Every other time I'd run in and grabbed his leg, Grandpa had laughed. Unbeknownst to me, he was going through alcohol withdrawal so bad that he was having delirium tremens (DTs) so this time was very different. He was hallucinating and thought I was the enemy from WWII coming to attack him. He didn't see me; he saw someone else. Even though he didn't have his prosthetic leg on, he caught me outside and tackled me. He was screaming and shoved homemade hot sauce down my throat. It was powerful enough to make a grown man cry. I screamed. Not only did I swallow it, it got all over my face and up my nostrils.

Thank God, Daddy was home and was able to get Grandpa off of me and snap him out of it. Grandpa felt bad and held me as he cried and apologized over and over. Then he left and started drinking again. I felt horrible. I didn't talk about the episode, but I blamed myself for everything that happened and his drinking again. The next two years, he was in and out of jail for drunken fights or drunk driving. When I was twelve, Grandpa succumbed to cirrhosis of the liver and went to be with Jesus. Two months prior, his youngest son, also an alcoholic, had committed suicide.

These deaths were a double whammy that took our once close family and tore it apart. People stopped talking and even moved to separate states. I blamed myself for Grandpa's death and thought everyone else did, too. Now, I know that's not true, but I felt that then. Our family didn't talk about emotions much, let alone know how to deal with them. It was always, "Get over it."

DAD IN CHARGE AT AGE TEN

Daddy's father had been in the Air Force and did more than a few tours in Vietnam. He was a carpenter in a Red Horse unit, a self-contained unit that had to take land that would be used as a base and then build the base. I don't even want to imagine what he saw and was required to do. He wasn't physically hurt, but he certainly had all the symptoms of PTSD.

My paternal grandparents had four kids and Daddy was the oldest. Grandpa was deployed a lot; Grandma was sick much of the time and had several miscarriages. By age ten, Daddy was taking care of his three younger siblings and had to be the man of the house when Grandpa was gone. His childhood was short-lived. They were stationed all over the world; by the time my dad graduated high school at age seventeen, he had been to thirteen different schools. They didn't have roots anywhere. They were never in a location long enough to have any real friends.

Daddy graduated while they were stationed in Spain and he returned to the United States to enlist in the Air Force. Grandpa retired at a base in California and the family finally got to settle in one place. My aunt and uncles got to go to high school there and developed real friendships for the first time.

Grandpa was very strict, as you might expect a military father would be. He seemed to be working all of the time and when he was at home, everything happened on a schedule. I'd go visit in the summer and I knew what time he ate breakfast, went to work, took a nap, ate supper, and ate ice cream at night. There wasn't much deviation. Even though I knew he loved us, he was distant and didn't show emotion often. He'd stare off in space like my mother's father had done and you knew he was mentally somewhere else. In Mom's family, her mother showed the love and held everyone together. In my dad's family, as long as you were obedient and didn't question anything, things were quiet. Even as a kid, I felt the frustration and resentment of my aunt and uncles toward their father. I was not sure exactly why, but he was very distant, even sitting in the same room with me. He was frustrated, too.

BOTH PARENTS SERVED

Every time my parents left on deployment, I was struck with fear. *Were they coming back? How long would they be gone this time? Will they be okay when they return? What will happen next?* Our home atmosphere was constant trauma and stress.

My dad got out of the military so my sister and I could have a place to call home and develop the lifelong friendships that he never had. I'm grateful for that. Short of moving so much, we grew up a lot like he did. I knew my dad loved me, but because of what he went through growing up, being injured in the military, and his own PTSD, he was hard and distant like his father was.

As long as you were obedient, didn't upset my mom, and did well in school, things were quiet at home. Daddy was taught to never, ever upset his mother, so that's what we were taught. I'm not talking about only staying out of trouble; we were also taught not to tell her anything that could upset her. That was really confusing as a kid. Out of fear of my dad, I couldn't really communicate with Mom. That pretty much meant that I wasn't telling her anything or having conversations that a daughter needs to have with her mother. I started to think that maybe she didn't love me and I didn't dare ask her about it. Totally not true, but I wondered.

DID "BOY" THINGS WITH DAD

My sister was the rebellious one and closer to Mom. I was the quiet one who stayed out of the way, got straight A's, and did anything I could to please my dad. He wanted a boy, but Mom couldn't have any more kids after me. I gladly did "boy" things to spend time with Daddy—sports, working on cars, fishing, whatever I could to be with him when he was home and make him proud of me. After Daddy got out of the Air Force, he still worked for them as a Department of Defense (DoD) civilian. He worked on top-secret projects and traveled like one would do in the military. We couldn't tell anyone about his job and were taught to be wary of anyone who asked.

We were taught to be vigilant, self-sufficient little soldiers. I was alone a lot, but I had my dog and could have fun anywhere, so I was happy. Daddy didn't know Jesus and Mom didn't go to church. Thankfully, we lived around my mom's family and Grandma made sure we went to church every Sunday. When I was a teenager, Daddy did accept Jesus and everything changed. He realized what Grandpa's PTSD had done to him and what his had done to us. He felt really bad and tried hard to change. Finally, I had a father I could talk to without fear. I was extremely grateful to God.

ENLISTED IN AIR FORCE

I enlisted in the Air Force in 1994 at age nineteen. I really wanted to stay home in California and be a K-9 officer with the sheriff's department, but Daddy wanted me to enlist, so once again, I obeyed him and left. Because of my family background, the military came as naturally to me as breathing. In basic training, I was the only one out of sixty-five women who didn't get in trouble and couldn't be made to cry. None of those drill instructors were scarier or tougher than Daddy.

Carmen and Rich Wilkinson both served in the Air Force.

My career field was non-destructive inspection (NDI), which meant I had to inspect aircraft for cracks and defects using X-ray, ultrasound, and other cool means. I absolutely loved it! Not only was I really good at it, I was also good at training others.

My husband, Rich, and I met shortly after getting to our first base at Charleston Air Force Base (AFB) in South Carolina. He came from a military family in Connecticut. In 1995, we were married and had our first son. Rich's career field was aircraft structural maintenance. He'd repair just about everything I found cracked or damaged and a lot more.

FIRST TO GET C-17 GLOBEMASTER

We were the first AFB to get the C-17 Globemaster cargo plane. Instead of having metal skin like most aircraft, almost all of it was made out of different composite materials, so we all had to learn how to inspect and repair it. We had short trips for training here and there, but nothing at the same time. In 1999, McChord AFB in Washington State was going to be the next base to get the C-17; Rich and I were chosen to transfer there to train our shops. We packed up our two little boys and moved across the country.

We were excited because we would be only twelve hours away from my parents and the boys would get to know them. Also, some of my mom's family had moved to Washington and we were excited to finally be living around family. We bought our first house and got everyone settled in. We spent the next two years working hard to get everyone at work trained and having fun with family when off-duty. We were blessed and life was great.

9/11 CHANGES EVERYTHING

Everything changed with the terrorist attacks of September 11, 2001. We were suddenly at war. We were used to normal peacetime Operations Security (OPSEC) and were now on high alert 24/7. Our sons thought it was cool to see all of the armored vehicles at the gates of the Air Force base, but the uncertainty of what might come through those gates was sinking in for the adults. We felt safe on base, but the forty-minute drive to our off-base home was often unnerving. Due to the very real threat of another attack anywhere in the United States— especially against the military and their families—our lives changed in more ways than I can explain.

It was easy to let fear overpower me when I was out in public and someone of Middle Eastern descent even looked at me, especially if I had the kids with me. The military trained us for many situations, but this was different. The number of people in my career field was small, so not only were we deploying with our jets, we supported the deployments of other bases when they had no one to send with our skill sets.

In 2001, I was deployed to a base in the Middle East. I thank God that my husband didn't have to deploy while I was gone and that his mother was able to help with the children. I'd never had to leave my kids like that and the fact that she was there kept me sane and able to do my job without worrying about what would happen if Rich got deployed when I was gone.

NO WEAPONS ALLOWED

I can't say where I was, but the people of that country didn't know we were officially there. Instead of the security of our own military base, we had to work on their base and live among civilians. We weren't even allowed to have weapons, which none of us had ever heard of. Our security only had flash-lights for protection. There was safety in numbers, but we weren't allowed to go anywhere in a big group. The few females in our group had orders to never go anywhere without four or five men with us. When we walked in public, I had our guys all around me like bodyguards.

Can you imagine? We were in a foreign country with no weapons. We had to assume that everyone there wanted to kill us—and most of them did. Just being an American made us walking targets. Being female made the situation even worse. A dog was held in higher regard than a woman. Then we found out that they think all American woman are whores—their words. Because of what they see on TV, they believe we are all allowed to have sex before marriage.

In 120-degree weather, I wore civilian clothes that covered everything except my hands and my face, but their men still tried to talk to me. Their grabbing hands often made their way through the guys around me no matter what. I found out much later that because my hair has red in it, the people were trying to touch me for a blessing of some kind. It still didn't make me feel better. Thinking about what would happen if they found out we were actually United States military and I was a Christian who wore a cross around my neck was almost too much to bear. I was terrified *all* of the time.

THE REALITY OF TERRORISM

From the comfort of home, Americans see whatever is shown on the news about Islamic terrorism in the Middle East. Believe me, the reality is far worse. When you have another human being look you in the eyes and you *know* they'd slit your throat and joyfully drag your body around the streets, it does something to you. I had never before seen or felt true evil like that. And this didn't happen just once; it happened every time we left our residence. Don't get me wrong, I do know they were not all like that. However, to maintain our safety in those situations, we had to be extremely aware and assume everyone was the enemy in order to stay alive and safe.

In certain places on our missions, we were subjected to sniper fire or surface-to-air missiles (SAMS). So, yeah, it was terrifying. Even though I was saved and baptized when I was ten, I only had head knowledge about Jesus and no real relationship with Him. I didn't walk in His peace like I now know I could have. If I had that close relationship with my Savior, a lot would have been different.

STAYING AT BLACKLISTED HOTEL

A few weeks before we were supposed to go home, we were moved into hotels so the next unit could settle in. However, from the minute I got into the hotel room, my phone rang off the hook with men asking if they could come up to visit. It was weird. My chief had me unplug my phone, but then the men came knocking at my door. I couldn't even feel safe in my room and couldn't open the door until my guys were there. No one understood it.

Then we discovered our hotel was on a blacklist and the military was not supposed to stay there. Apparently, European women came there on holiday and used it as a brothel. We finally understood why the local men were relentless. Because I was white and staying at this notorious hotel, they thought I was there looking for men. Needless to say, after what happened to me, the officials made sure no one stayed there again. Actually, in many places, military personnel are discouraged from going out in public anymore, thank God.

The last week we were there, we were allowed to go to one of the hotel restaurants and have a drink if we wanted. It was great to see everyone having a meal together and feeling somewhat normal. A few local men kept trying to buy drinks for me, but not only were we not allowed to accept anything, I wasn't drinking. I'd smile and say, "Thank you, I don't drink." I was offending them, but I was following orders as politely as possible. I got so caught up in our first real social gathering in a long time that I got comfortable for a moment. I had to use the restroom. Even though I knew I had a direct order not to go anywhere alone, in all of the excitement, I got up and went by myself.

ATTACKED BY THREE MEN

Three men who had tried to send drinks my way must have been watching because before I even got to a stall, they were in there and pushed me to the ground. It happened *so* fast! They held me down so tightly that I couldn't defend myself, let alone get away. I could barely scream. Thank God, the hotel security guard, armed with an AK-47, ran in and the men ran away. Had he not come, they would have all raped me and possibly killed me.

I did not want to tell my guys what had just happened, especially those who had been drinking, because it could have turned into an international incident. And it all happened so fast, I was in shock. The guard took me back to my room in a service elevator. Not long afterward, my girlfriend noticed my absence at the restaurant and came looking for me. I told her what happened, but I didn't want to tell anyone else. No matter what those men did to me, I was scared because I'd disobeyed a direct order. I'd never done that before. Immediately, I started condemning myself. I believed it wouldn't have happened had I not been complacent. It's sad when a woman can't go to the restroom without getting attacked.

The next day, my friend told our first sergeant and I was called into the commander's office. I'm glad she did it now, but at the time I thought, *That's it—my career is over.* But that's not what happened at all. Yes, they were mad because I went to the restroom alone, but they didn't charge me with anything. The government found the men who had assaulted me and wanted me to stay for their trial. Because that process could have taken six months to a year, I declined. I just wanted to go home.

BECOMING WHAT YOU HATE

One of our team was assigned to watch over me and guard the door. Hanging out one night, I let myself get talked into having a few drinks. I was with a different base and didn't know this man well, but I felt safe enough to go out. I was wrong. Just when I thought things couldn't get any worse, they did. He took advantage of the situation and I then became one of the military adulterers I hated.

I knew so many people who cheated on their spouses while deployed. I felt like one of them and couldn't tell anyone what happened. When alcohol is involved, people say the servicewoman *wanted* it and chalk it up to just another alcohol-related incident. I can't put into words how dirty and worthless I felt. *What was I going to tell my husband?!* Emotionally, this last incident hurt more than the local men attacking me. This was one of my *brothers*. I was angry and didn't trust anyone anymore.

We went home soon after that incident. I was excited to be back with my family and work around *my* people again. I thought I could forget about the bad events of the deployment and "get over it." No one told my command what happened, so I didn't have to talk about it. No matter how I tried, I still came back a different person. If anyone came close to touch me, even my husband or kids, I would jump away with a clenched fist. I thought it would fade away with time, but it only got worse.

Finally, I had to explain to my husband why I was so jumpy. I don't remember how long it took to tell him, but all of my fears were completely unwarranted. He wasn't mad at me; he was mad at the Air Force for putting me in that situation. Even though he'd tell me it wasn't my fault and I needed to give myself grace, I didn't know how to do that. I tried to keep moving forward and pretend that whole deployment didn't happen, but I couldn't get away from that nightmare.

While we were deployed, the mosques would broadcast their prayers from loudspeakers five times every day. We were bombing the Middle East and *none* of those prayers ever sounded pleasant. I couldn't understand what they were saying, but they yelled and sounded very angry.

LIVING IN A NIGHTMARE

Even being at home, if I heard anyone speaking Arabic, my mind would send me right back to the Middle East. I couldn't watch the news, listen to stories from guys at work, watch a movie with anything remotely Middle Eastern, or even watch my family play their video games. I was still living a horrible nightmare. I was unable to ignore or erase those memories.

Many servicemen and women who come back from deployment go to the doctor for the same complaints and symptoms. Then they end up with a medical board hearing and have to resign from their military careers. I absolutely didn't want that.

I worried about being deployed again. In my mental state, I knew I would have a very difficult time keeping things together. Instead, I joined the thousands of military personnel who suffer in silence because they don't want to leave the service.

DAUGHTER IS BORN

In 2002, we got pregnant and had our daughter. Rich and I talked about my discharge while I was pregnant. When a woman in the service gets pregnant, she has the choice to get out right up to the moment of birth. I didn't want to leave my family again, but I didn't know who I was without being in the Air Force. I thought everything would get better with the birth of my daughter. Even though I was so happy to have her, having my hormones out of sorts didn't help anything.

My anxiety and panic were out of control. I finally went to the doctor, who thought I had postpartum depression. I knew my problems were not that simple. They put me on depression and anxiety medications, but those made me feel horrible and emotionless, so I didn't take them.

Two months after I gave birth, I was told I had to deploy again. I was still on a maternity profile, not even cleared to fully do my job yet. But many people in my shop were already deployed and the only option was to send my boss or me. I didn't even get clearance from the doctor first. We were at war. I did not think I had any choice.

Thank God, my mother in-law came to the rescue again. My body wasn't ready to work out yet, let alone do the lifting that my job entails. I also felt tremendous guilt for leaving my sons again and a brand-new baby daughter. Would my beautiful little girl even remember me when I got home?

Carmen inspected C-17 Globemaster cargo planes like this one.
(U.S. Air Force photo by Airman 1st Class Marcus M. Bullock)

LIFTING 200-POUND WHEELS

Part of my job was to inspect the C-17 landing gear wheels when the tires were changed. These weigh over two hundred pounds each. When at home base, there are usually other people to help with lifting heavy objects. For safety reasons, we weren't supposed to lift anything over forty pounds by ourselves, but I spent entire shifts moving and inspecting wheels. Sometimes, there would be someone to help me, but most of the time, I was alone. I had to do what was necessary to keep the mission going and this was no different, post-baby or not.

The damage done to my spine on that deployment was serious. When I came home, I couldn't even hold my baby without feeling excruciating pain. While the doctors tried to figure out what to do with me, they put me on pain medications and muscle relaxers. I did every physical therapy they offered, but my condition only got worse. It got to the point where I was in a wheelchair because of pinched nerves that would make my legs go numb or give out at any moment. If I didn't feel worthless enough.....

By the time I was able to have back surgery, the only thing they could do was remove the four bulging damaged discs because there wasn't anything solid to fuse the discs to. The Air Force deemed me unfit for military service with no chance of recovery. They offered me a severance, but we fought for a medical retirement. It took a while and we had to go to court, but we finally won. I was officially retired.

PROGNOSIS DISCOURAGING

Doctors gave me no encouragement for any healing or recovery. They had no answers either. Each time I saw a doctor, things remained the same. My multiple prescriptions would get renewed and I would be sent home. They continued to label me 100 percent disabled with further deterioration likely in the future.

It was a very stressful time and the emotional trauma was overwhelming. I felt I had let everyone down, including myself, my family, and my country. I know it's not true now, but then, I thought God must have been punishing me for what happened overseas and for not getting out when I had the chance. Condemnation and self-hate were very real and very strong. Somehow, I had to learn how to live as a wife and mother not only with raw, damaged emotions, but also physically broken. My husband and kids were great about everything, so helpful and loving. I was the one hating myself and getting bitter.

After my twelve years of faithful service, I was *so* mad and hurt at the Air Force! Not only for what happened overseas, but for spitting me out when I was hurt. I knew people who were allowed to stay in the service even though they couldn't deploy. I knew I could still train people, but it didn't seem to matter. I got set up with the Veterans Administration (VA) and was deemed 100 percent permanently disabled with a medical retirement.

RECEIVES A WHEELCHAIR

By that time, I had so many more conditions that they said they'd never even evaluate me again. They believed there was no chance I would ever get better in any area. They gave me an electric wheelchair and told us that eventually, I wouldn't even be able to walk, that I would be in that chair forever. I told them I wouldn't accept that diagnosis. I wanted to get better.

I knew Jesus could heal me, but I never asked Him. I felt so unworthy that I wouldn't even ask the Lord to heal me. I didn't feel I even deserved to ask. Life went on and we did the best we could.

In 2006, my sister went to heaven. Three months later, so did Daddy. Both deaths were unexpected. Grief like I couldn't imagine swept in on top of everything else. Other than Rich, they had been my support, the only people I could talk to about anything. I didn't get a chance to grieve because I had to help my mom. While being there for everyone else who was grieving, I didn't allow myself to work through the process.

Daddy passed while the kids and I were at their house visiting for the summer. Rich had gotten orders to go to Korea for a year and Daddy was going to take care of us. Now I needed Rich more than ever and he was still in the Air Force in Washington. We went to Congress twice to get a year's deferment on his orders, but they said "no" both times. After fifteen years of service and so close to retirement, Rich went to the McChord AFB commander and asked to get out. Rich explained that his family was more important and he got permission to be discharged. Although I was relieved because we'd be together again, I felt guilty that he had to leave the Air Force because of me. He made that choice out of love, but again, I condemned myself.

MOVED TO CONNECTICUT

We decided to move to Connecticut, where Rich grew up, and my mom chose to join us. We wanted the kids to have roots and develop lifelong friends. We promised the children we would stay put and stop the frequent moves. The Lord blessed us with a wonderful home, a great job for Rich, and wonderful blue-ribbon schools for the kids.

Everyone was making friends and flourishing except me, but I did my best to show everyone a happy face. I didn't know anyone and didn't try to make any friends. I thought as long as I had my family, I didn't need anyone else. I wanted to be the class mom and do things with the kids that I used to, but I just couldn't. Rich and the kids were doing great and that's all I cared about. The kids made friends and played lots of sports.

Sporting events or doctors' appointments at the VA were pretty much the only times I left the house. We bought our German Shepherd, Gunner, from our neighbors, who were horse and dog breeders at a nearby farm. They were my only friends. Even with an alarm system on the house and a 120-pound dog, I was scared when Rich wasn't home. I didn't understand what was happening to me, but the more I isolated and condemned myself, the worse I became. I'd always been a happy person—in fact, people often called me "Sunshine"—until this happened. My only reprieve from myself was when my family was home or when I was spending time at the neighbors' farm with the horses and dogs. It felt strange to me, but my house was the *only* place I felt safe with my dog at my side and the security alarm on. This same safe haven also became my prison.

GIVEN MORE MEDICATIONS

Even though they are educated on veterans' medical issues, the VA didn't know how to treat my PTSD or anything else. More medications were prescribed, which simply made things worse. I'd always had a high tolerance for pain, but my constant discomfort got to the point where I was in severe pain all of the time. I had fibromyalgia, debilitating migraines over half of the time, and on and on.

No amount of narcotics ever took away my pain. At one point, they had me on 180 milligrams of morphine three times a day, plus Vicodin, muscle relaxers, and so much more that I don't even remember. Every month, we left the VA pharmacy with a brown paper grocery bag full of medications. I knew the meds would eventually kill me if I took them all. I got myself to the point where I was only taking enough morphine, muscle relaxer, and Motrin to be able to get out of bed.

On a good day, I could do some laundry, tidy up the kitchen, and cook supper. Before I got hurt, I'd decorate the house and keep it clean. I loved yardwork, too. Now I could barely do anything and Rich not only had to manage a full-time job, but do what I couldn't do around the house as well.

Rich was and *is* amazing. He went on school field trips with the kids and really tried to do it all.

Over the years, Rich did more and more for me and it made me feel terrible. This entire situation drastically changed our relationship. Overnight, he went from being my best friend and husband to my full-time caregiver. This change also affected our marriage relationship and neither of us knew what to do for the other anymore.

MAJOR DAMAGE TO BODY

I was pushing myself so hard that I was creating more damage to my body. In 2010, I had to have all of my teeth pulled, get dentures, have a complete hysterectomy, and a bladder mesh put in. The doctors couldn't find medical reasons why I kept getting cavities and abscesses at the gumline, why the blood stopped flowing in my uterus and backed up in my veins, or why my bladder leaked so much.

Finally, they said it must be spinal cord damage and Gulf War Syndrome because of what I had been exposed to in the Middle East. According to them, all of those surgeries were my only option. I already felt bad enough about myself and had to accept that I would never get better, only worse. That's when I stopped trying.

While Rich and the kids were at work and school, I laid on the couch all day and watched TV. I never slept more than an hour at a time so I was exhausted to boot. I started to sleep on the couch because I didn't want to disturb Rich with my restless nights. For ten years, I couldn't remember ever dreaming, but I would wake up gasping for air like someone was trying to suffocate me. My animals would even wake me up and I'd have to catch my breath. The only explanation the VA gave me was I must have had night terrors.

FEELING ANCIENT...AND BROKEN

My hormones were so messed up that I had no sex drive anymore. I felt like an ancient old woman. I couldn't keep the house clean and stopped expecting Rich to do any of it, so I wouldn't let anyone come over to visit either. I thought I was saving the kids from embarrassment, but all it did was rob them of fun times with their friends at our house. My pride isolated me even more. Rich was never an entertainer so he didn't mind not having people over. I should have asked the kids to do chores to help me, but I felt so guilty about being broken that I didn't. Soon, I couldn't sit, stand, or walk more than ten minutes at a time. Lifting a gallon of milk was impossible and I couldn't leave my house.

Rich was officially considered my caregiver through the VA. If any VA workers needed to come to the house, Rich had to take time off work to come home. He had to take unpaid time off to take me to the doctor's office too, which was happening too often. Losing that income didn't help the situation. I was so scared and hypervigilant that I couldn't go inside a building unless I knew where all of the exits were. After about ten minutes, I'd panic and couldn't breathe until I went outside.

LIVING WITH MOUNTING FEAR

The more physically disabled I became, the more fearful I was. I couldn't do anything without Rich's presence and support. I knew I couldn't defend myself and I had irrational fears. When we were invited to parties or events, Rich and the kids went without me because I just couldn't go. Even though I wanted to go, fear would grip me and I'd get sick.

My mom, Grandma, and extended family worried about me all of the time and wondered if I'd die from the meds or possibly take my own life. I never wanted to kill myself, but there were many days that I wasn't too happy about waking up. Rich and the kids even had to be trained on how to administer Narcan because the VA said there was a possibility that I would go to sleep and not wake up. How terrifying for them! I was stuck in my own personal hell and had no idea how to get out of it.

I wanted to go to church, but that meant leaving the house. Thank God I was able to watch Joel Osteen, Joyce Meyer, and Joseph Prince on TV. I didn't understand why, but the PTSD got so bad that I couldn't even read and comprehend one sentence at a time. I had been a straight-A student and now Rich had to read and fill out forms for me. I was paralyzed with fear and hope wasn't in my vocabulary.

HEARING FROM THE ENEMY

The enemy would continuously whisper in my ear: "Your family would be better without you. Your husband deserves a new wife. They don't want you. They don't need you like this."

I honestly got to the point where I thought that Rich *would* be better off with a new wife and the kids needed a new mom who could function. Even though no one said those things or ever tried to make me feel bad, that's what

I thought. I loved and treasured time with Rich and the kids, but was tormented any time I was alone. I felt so unworthy that I didn't even pray for myself or ask God to help me, only my family.

I couldn't imagine what my grandfathers had gone through during their deployments, but I started to understand what they went through when they returned home. Those traumatic memories came in like a flood and the feelings of shame, guilt, and fear overwhelmed me. *Now* I understood why someone would try to escape with drugs or alcohol, or keep so busy with work that they didn't have time to think about their past. I experienced the same type of breathtaking anxiety and panic attacks that they had fought through as well as the frustration of not knowing why or how to get better. Hopelessness paralyzed my life.

GOD SENDS A MESSAGE

Then one night in early 2018, I'd fallen asleep watching the news and woke up hearing my Daddy's voice in my right ear. Twice, I heard him say, "Baby girl, this isn't you! Get off your butt!" Friends, I jumped to attention and I *really* thought he'd be standing there when I opened my eyes.

Daddy wasn't there, of course, but from that moment, it was like God took blinders off of me and I *knew* that I needed a relationship with Jesus. I didn't understand it, but God knew I needed to wake up. I was in *awe*! I had never cried out to Him with words, but He heard my groans. He had truly left the ninety-nine sheep to rescue one—me! (See Matthew 18:12–14; Luke 15:3–7.)

I still couldn't read, so I couldn't read my Bible, but the Lord led me to wonderful men and women of God on YouTube. I don't think I slept for a week after that. One of the first people he led me to was Katie Souza, who taught about healing soul wounds. God also led me to Joan Hunter and I watched her pray for people and saw Jesus heal them. I'd never seen anyone lay hands on someone else for healing, let alone seen a miracle like that.

LED TO CONFERENCE IN PHOENIX

Sometime later, God led me to Patricia King and a promotional video for the Women on the Front Lines World Conference in Phoenix, Arizona. I *knew* that God wanted me to go. To my surprise, many of the people I had been watching on TV were speaking at the conference. I talked to Rich about it and he reluctantly agreed to let me go because my mom could go with me and he was unable to go.

To my knowledge, God had never told me to do anything or go anywhere before. I didn't know what to expect, but I wasn't feeling afraid, and that surprised both me and Rich. During my entire life, I had viewed God like I did my grandfathers and my Daddy. I knew in my head that God loved me because He sent Jesus to die for me, but I thought He was distant and only happy with me if and when I did everything right. I thought that I had blown it with God and He was punishing me.

Now I know these were *all* lies from hell. The enemy tried very hard to stop me from going, but I persevered. I didn't know what to expect because I'd never been to a conference like that before, but I was so excited. For the first time in forever, I had hope that something could get better, even just one thing.

MIRACULOUS HEALING WITH JOAN

Joan Hunter prays for Carmen Wilkinson

The first day of the conference on July 26, 2018, started with Joan Hunter as the first speaker. I was the first person to be prayed for. She had a word of knowledge about a neck injury and asked if anyone had lost height. My hand went up like lightning and she called me up on stage.

Mama just about pushed me out in the aisle with excitement. Joan prayed for Jesus to give me new discs in my back and restore the height I had lost. I was looking at her while she was praying and I heard over a thousand women gasp at the same time. I didn't feel anything when she prayed and I thought, *I wonder what just happened.* I remember Joan saying something about me growing, but I didn't feel anything. Then she prayed for trauma to go and removed the label of PTSD from me.

Sometimes, I would feel someone's hands around my neck. I would wake up at night feeling like I was being strangled. Joan explained that was cellular memory of an incident in my past. She put her hands around my neck that day and commanded the feeling and the cellular memory to go. That feeling has never come back!

Joan asked me how I felt and I remember saying, "I don't know." Then I bent over and touched my toes. I hadn't been able to do that in fifteen years. I was in shock and didn't know what God had just done. Because the conference was being livestreamed, I got to watch the replay after the session was over. I watched myself grow four inches! That's why everyone had gasped. I sent the video to my husband right away and he wasn't sure he could believe his eyes.

HOLY SPIRIT BAPTISM

That night during the evening session, I received the baptism of the Holy Spirit. For the first time in years, I slept comfortably. I woke up sweating so profusely that I had to change my clothes three times that night. I didn't understand it, but I knew that whatever God was doing was awesome.

The next morning, I knew that I was free from PTSD and Jesus had cleansed my heart. Overnight, I went from thinking we should do the world a favor and drop a bomb on the Middle East to having a heart of compassion toward them and wanting them to know Jesus. I had joy and hope again. Twelve years of grief over my sister and Daddy was gone; I was a new person. I'm so grateful to Jesus for having mercy on me and setting me free.

The next morning, in between sessions, I saw Joan talking to someone in the hallway. I told Mom, "I know it was Jesus who healed me, but I wish I could thank her and tell her that my PTSD is gone. My heart changed overnight. I don't want to bug her though. I'm sure a lot of people do."

My mom stopped, grabbed my arm, and said, "You get yourself over there right now. I won't let you pass her by."

MOM IS ALSO SET FREE

My visit with Joan was so cool. She asked if she could record my testimony, so we did that while Mom waited on a bench about ten feet away. After we were done, I told Joan how sad my mom was since Daddy and my sister went to heaven and asked if Joan could pray for Mom. I got to witness Jesus heal and set my mom free, too. Her shoulders went from hunched forward to standing tall—so tall that her shirt wasn't covering her belly anymore.

Mom said, "I'm gonna need to go shopping." She walked out of there full of joy and twirling her cane instead of depending on it. She didn't need hearing aids anymore either, and she was set free from her PTSD and grief. Thank You, Jesus!

I didn't think I was worthy of getting healed. I never asked God to heal me until that day when I realized He truly wanted to knock that trauma off of me once and for all. God healed my shoulders during worship another day of the conference. Due to a work injury, my arms would go numb if I tried to raise them, but now, I could lift them high to worship my Jesus. Hallelujah!

SPREADING THE GOOD NEWS

Since that day, life has never been the same. All I want to do is tell everyone what Jesus has done, lay hands on people, and see them healed and delivered too. Before we left the conference, I bought Joan's healing school curriculum. When I got home and told my family what happened, they didn't know how to accept it or even believe it.

Since the day I got home, I've slept in bed with my husband. After I lay my head on the pillow, I'm asleep in less than two minutes and I sleep all night. I dream again and don't wake up gasping for air. After meeting Joan, the PTSD, the pain, and the fibromyalgia are all gone. Fifty pounds melted off me in three and a half months. The wall I had built up disappeared. The 24/7 tormenting fear is shattered and gone. I can play with my kids again. I can enjoy my husband again without pain or shame. I can cook, clean, do yardwork, walk the dog—everything. I am *alive* again.

At first, my family wasn't sure Jesus really healed me. They were waiting for the other shoe to drop. They expected me to go back to the way I was for so long. That's *never* happening and they're slowly seeing that my healing is real. My husband has gotten his *new* wife, a better wife than he ever knew before. The kids are getting to know a healed Mama, some for the first time.

GOD REVEALS HIS LOVE

God is also healing my family from the trauma and restoring us in many ways. I was able to travel to California to visit my family, all by myself. I had doubted that I would ever get to see them again. I got to share my testimony with them and now they have faith that God will heal them too.

God is revealing His love for me and healing me more and more every day. He's peeling me like an onion and showing me who and what I need to forgive and release, including myself. He's helping me with every step and I'm filled with gratitude.

I am actually getting in touch with my feminine side. I enjoy wearing nice clothes, using makeup, and the weight loss. One day, I actually thought

I looked cute, which thoroughly surprised me because I had never thought about that before.

In the last year, I've been able to travel to meetings in four different states. Of course, I use wisdom, but I am not trapped by fear. I *know* God is with me and won't ever leave me. He led me to Engaging Heaven Church in New London, Connecticut, and I'm so excited to have a church family.

With the help of my doctor, I was able to get off of all of the medications. Now the only thing I'm addicted to is Jesus.

HEALING SCHOOL GRADUATE

Last month, I had the honor of going to Joan Hunter Ministries in Tomball, Texas. I went through her Healing School, was ordained, and graduated on September 21, 2019, which was Daddy's birthday. I know he was cheering me on from heaven.

Now I can minister healing to others. I received a prophetic word and I want to set the captives free. By studying and preparing for ordination, I learned much about God, His love, and myself.

I am praying for people and spreading God's love everywhere,

Carmen Wilkinson

whether it's at the store, a gas station, the doctor's office, church, or on the prayer team at a conference with Joan. God is kicking the enemy in the teeth every day with my life and I'm thankful and grateful.

I am so happy to be able to minister to other family members who have suffered from PTSD, both veterans and first responders. I am now able and equipped to help my family get healed from their PTSD. I sleep under a "Miracles Happen! for Veterans" blanket every night and can feel additional healing every day. I have given these blankets to several family members. I want them to experience God's miracles just like I did.

I loved being in the military until my world crashed around me. Today, I want to touch the people who the world writes off as hopeless, including my veteran brothers and sisters, prisoners, mental patients, addicts, and everyone else who is hurting. I'll go into any darkness with my Jesus. He's given me a second chance and I won't squander it. I'm not sure what He has in store for me and my family, but whatever it is, it's going to be awesome. In the meantime, I'm learning to rest in Him and have an intimacy with Him that I never knew was possible.

THOUSANDS FEEL HOPELESS

Today, thousands of veterans are in the same hopeless position that had me trapped for so long. Many marriages are irreparably damaged and divorce often follows. People attempt to find relief and some control using alcohol, drugs, vigorous exercise, or other means. However, God is waiting to help every one of these hurting, damaged men and women. I plan on introducing everyone I can to my Jesus, who healed and restored my life, my soul, and my family.

In His presence *is* fullness of joy and that's where I want to live from and be forever. Everything has changed so fast and so drastically that I find myself saying, "Is this really happening?" And yes it is! Hallelujah!

—Carmen Wilkinson

12

JARED LASKEY

PTSD and Traumatic Brain Injury

It is my pleasure to share my story with you, warrior. First off, welcome home—*welcome home!* Thank you for your sacrifice. And thank you for continuing the fight. We need you healed and whole because no one else can do what God has called you to do.

Perhaps you need to hear that or maybe you'll brush that off, but I am grateful for you because I have walked in your boots. I have also walked through my own nightmare. The war at home is just as real as what you have been through serving our country. The battle for our mind is one of the most difficult battles we fight. It bleeds over into our relationships, families, holidays, workplaces, and more.

It seemed to be so much easier being over there—the rush of adrenaline, the brotherhood, and the camaraderie. The world back home doesn't understand what we've been through. But that's okay; you protected their way of life even if they can't understand the pain and turmoil you went through. Very few will ever understand your fighting was to keep your team members on your right and left alive.

SERVED 2006–2011

My name is Jared Laskey and I am a Marine. I served from October 2006 to August 2011 as a field radio operator with the infantry of Second Battalion, Eighth Marines, stationed in Camp Lejeune, North Carolina. I deployed to Ramadi, Iraq, from October 2007 through May 2008 and Helmand Province, Afghanistan, from May to November 2009.

My platoon completed over one hundred combat missions in Afghanistan, protecting the battalion commander and other government dignitaries, ambassadors, and generals, such as Gen. David Petraeus and even senators like John Kerry when they came to our area of operations. As a mobile platoon, we would relieve platoons on the *front lines* even though the lines were blurred. We would hold security around patrol bases being built, go on foot patrols to retrieve assets and personnel, do mine sweeping operations, and more.

Out of my platoon of twenty-six Marines with one Navy corpsman, sixteen were blown up. The rest of us made it home alive, but we were all changed. I was never blown up, but every improvised explosive device that hit my platoon exploded while I was driving the MaxxPro just behind the vehicle that was hit.

Looking back on it now, on July 6, 2009, we were on a mission, taking the battalion commander, Lt. Col. Christian Cabaniss, and other officers to the front after Operation Khanjari kicked off for the *summer of decision*, when the locals would vote for the first time in forever.

We were told that Route Cowboys was cleared a day or two before by the combat engineers. And I didn't doubt that it was, but as we continued driving past a patrol base, everything got eerily quiet. Maybe you know that quietness, that stillness. I had first experienced it several weeks before when we all knew enemy contact was imminent. The only thing you can hear is your own breathing and then the adrenaline rush kicks in.

"I DON'T LIKE THIS"

On this day, while driving in the complete silence, I looked at my staff sergeant, who was my vehicle commander. "I don't like this," I said.

He looked at me and said, "What?" Then he looked forward where I was looking. And right then, the lead vehicle hit an IED. The explosion, the sound, the debris flying every direction while I questioned whether my friends were alive or not—all will forever be etched into my memory.

In time, the longer I was *in country*, the more I became numb to everything. In a way, I had to die in order to survive. I always had my faith in Jesus and saw God do amazing things through me. From time to time, I would lead Bible studies. But even though He lived in me, my soul was dying and I didn't realize it at the time.

While on deployment, a young Marine had a negligent discharge of a shotgun inside my truck. The blast and impact were near my head. When it first happened, I thought we were mortared as it struck the machine gun turret. But soon afterward, we saw the shotgun in the lance corporal's hands and figured it out. He ended up in a lot of trouble. I thought I could brush off the headaches I experienced. The corpsman kept watch on me through the rest of the deployment, but my real problems didn't show up until after we returned home.

JOYFUL HOMECOMING

It was the day before Thanksgiving 2009. The moment I stepped off the bus, my wife, Rochelle, handed my six-month-old twins to me. I was ecstatic and overjoyed. They were born thirteen days into my deployment and were on my mind every day. Even in combat, thoughts of them and my four-year-old son rushed through my mind.

Returning home, it seemed like I had a new lease on life. I laughed quite a bit and my wife and sister-in-law said they loved the *new* Jared. It was fun for a while. Soon after Christmas, I felt empty. After the New Year started, anger began to flare up and focusing on things was difficult. I became an emotional roller coaster. One moment I'd be happy and the next, I would be putting a junior Marine on blast. I felt like I was losing control of my mind while standing on the brink of hell's flames.

I called out to God but couldn't sense or feel Him. I had to rely on faith. My anger boiled over and my wife knew something was wrong. Unfortunately, she was affected as my rage and depression escalated. I knew I needed help because I wanted to die. I wanted a sniper to shoot me so I could be relieved and no longer be a burden to the ones I loved. Love, joy, and peace felt a universe away during this time in my life.

The *combat cocktail* came my way as I was diagnosed with post-traumatic stress disorder (PTSD) and traumatic brain injury (TBI). Multiple prescriptions, plus the back pain from the load we carried, the selective serotonin reuptake inhibitors (antidepressants) and therapies were a route to becoming a zombie.

I felt like a waste of space, going from appointment to appointment, being told my days as a Marine were over. A diagnosis of PTSD back then meant a physical evaluation board to either medically separate or medically retire you. But I held on to my faith, calling on Jesus, and trying to make it work with my wife and kids.

You and I are warriors. And as warriors, we know how to fight. So I fought hard for my sanity as I said, "I left part of my brain in Helmand."

My wife and I fought for our marriage and family. She stuck next to me, beating the odds that 80 percent of combat veterans divorce. Some studies show the divorce rate for combat veterans at 95 percent! But my wife understood the power of prayer and would not relent as she stood on the promises of God. And for that I am eternally grateful for her.

THERAPY AND JESUS

When weird therapies were offered, I declined, knowing I needed to return to the basics of spiritual growth. I threw myself into God, prayer, biblical meditation, memorization, and serving in a church.

When God opened doors for me to serve in ministry in 2011, I knew I needed to pursue inner healing, so I went to a Sozo prayer group at my friend Michael Rogers's church in New Bern, North Carolina. What I encountered through that prayer was incredible and I was healed of my migraine headaches from TBI. I still fought the PTSD, but I celebrated that I was healed of migraines and in the process of healing. I was even trained in Sozo and inner healing prayer, which complemented my prophetic gifts. I would even do "self Sozo" when bad memories came to mind.

I believe in the finished work of the cross, that God can heal immediately and we are not to bring up the past. But sometimes, the past has a way of hijacking us and invading in the most inopportune times. So we are to take those thoughts captive and heal memories under the care of Jesus as He brings them to light. Over the years, I weaned myself off medications.

To help discipline my mind, I immersed myself in seminary studies. It was still a battle, but God was winning the war. Soon after completing my master of divinity, I got a part-time job working with private military contractors and agencies preparing for deployments. The rush of adrenaline at work showed me I should have done this sooner as it made me feel good and part of a cause bigger than myself again.

WELCOME HOME INITIATIVE

Then in November 2018, my wife registered us for the Welcome Home Initiative in Virginia Beach. This weekend retreat was close to home. It emphasized inner healing for combat veterans and their spouses. For some reason, a memory from combat haunted me. I saw our Navy corpsman trying to stop a seventeen-year-old Taliban fighter from bleeding out after a firefight.

Even though I would surrender this memory to Jesus, it still kept haunting me.

I distinctly remember watching them work on him and I felt nothing. For that, I was ashamed because I was wounded morally. As a Christian, I told myself I should have a feeling of compassion, but at that time, I was too numb, too dead on the inside to feel anything during deployment. However, since the memory kept crashing in and interfering in my civilian life, I knew I had to deal with it head-on as a warrior.

I had been making a chain of prayer over the years, receiving prayer from friends and family, itinerant ministers, and more. Like a warrior, I was contending for total healing. Right before the weekend started, my friend Scott Gilbert prayed over my mind, agreeing in prayer with me that I would be healed of PTSD and all its effects.

Father Nigel Mumford is a combat veteran and Spirit-filled Anglican priest who was mentored in healing by Francis MacNutt. He started By His Wounds Ministry to help bring healing to combat veterans.

PRAYER FOR HEALING

I was the first to volunteer for prayer among the combat veterans that weekend. Among them were not only veterans of Iraq and Afghanistan, but also some Vietnam veterans. Many were on their second or third marriages, but were there for help to break the cycle of despair, depression, rage, and everything else that comes with the invisible wounds of war.

As Nigel prayed and I spoke out the memory, in a vision, the scene changed. In my mind, the Navy doctor working on the young Taliban became Jesus. He looked up at me with His eyes full of comfort. Jesus lovingly said, "I see you, My son."

In that instant, a huge burden lifted from me. I relaxed and felt such peace. I left the retreat feeling renewed. Within the next few weeks, I realized I was no longer taking my

Jared Laskey

medication. I'd weaned myself from twelve prescriptions down to one over the last few years. Suddenly, I didn't need it. I was healed!

Even though there was still some anxiety afterwards, I decided to start the ketogenic diet, which I knew was helping a close family friend's daughter who had neurological issues. Since PTSD is connected neurologically, I knew it couldn't hurt to try it out. The fog and anxiety lifted as I pursued God's presence and started exercising, first walking and later running, then joining a Christian martial arts dojo. I lost sixty pounds and am now in the best shape of my life while still spiking my adrenaline from time to time through exercise and the work I do.

I attribute the miracles and healing to Jesus. He is the same yesterday, today, and forever. And as He healed me, sometimes instantaneously and sometimes through a process, He can also heal you. He loves you so much. It does take hard work at times. It's a daily choice to combat PTSD, work on relationships, pray, meditate on God's Word, and renew the mind. Ask for and receive prayer and build a chain of healing. You and I are warriors. We've been through worse. And Jesus heals.

JESUS IS A WARRIOR

That is my journey to being healed of PTSD and TBI. In the future, I will write more of my story. But for now, it is my hope and prayer that you're encouraged and see that there is light at the end of the tunnel. There is hope in spite of the feeling of hopelessness. There is joy and laughter again for you. There is success and victory waiting for you. The rules of engagement and warfare are different today. However, you are still a warrior and as a warrior, Jesus is fighting with you and for you.

Welcome home!

Then I saw heaven opened, and behold, a white horse! The one sitting on it is called Faithful and True, and in righteousness he judges and makes war. His eyes are like a flame of fire, and on his head are many diadems, and he has a name written that no one knows but himself. He is clothed in a robe dipped in blood, and the name by which he is called is The Word of God. And the armies of heaven, arrayed in fine linen, white and pure, were following him on white horses. From his mouth comes a sharp sword with which to strike down the nations, and he will rule them with a rod of iron. He will tread the winepress of the fury of the wrath of God the

Almighty. On his robe and on his thigh he has a name written, King of kings and Lord of lords. (Revelation 19:11–16 ESV)

YOUR ROAD TO HEALING

Your road to total healing should include:

+ Daily spiritual disciplines—the secret place of prayer, biblical meditation, memorization, renewing the mind, fasting, and fellowship.

+ Make a chain of prayer—receive prayer from ministers, friends, and family agreeing that you are healed in Jesus's name. Look back on those prayers and see the chain you are developing of people agreeing and standing on God's Word with you.

+ Take captive every thought and make it obedient to Christ. When bad memories intrude and invade, surrender each one to Jesus and ask Him to show you where He is in your memory. Focus on Him.

+ Exercise—find the fitness plan that is best for you. Talk to a doctor or fitness coach.

+ Adrenaline—during deployment, this spiked constantly. On your return home, you may have experienced adrenal fatigue. Find something that spikes your adrenaline from time to time.

+ Healthy diet—for me, it is the keto diet because it helps many neurological disorders. Talk to your doctor or physician to determine the diet that will work best for you.

Jared Laskey is the host of "Adventures in the Spirit" podcast on the Charisma Podcast Network. He has been a contributing writer for FaithWire News, God TV, Charisma Magazine, AG News, Message of the Open Bible, and more. He holds a B.S. in Pastoral Studies from Eugene Bible College in Oregon, an M.A. in Christian Ministry from Shepherds Theological Seminary in North Carolina, and Master of Divinity from Regent University in Virginia. He served in the United States Marine Corps from 2006 through 2011, deploying to Iraq in 2007-2008 and Afghanistan in 2009. His heart and passion is to awaken this generation to the power of the Holy Spirit. Using his prophetic gifts to glorify Jesus, he teaches people how to hear God's voice and pursue intimacy with Him and helps to bring healing to veterans. Visit Jared's website: www.firebornministries.com.

13

RENEE NICKELL

Suicidal Thoughts, PTSD, and Depression

When I look back on my life, some of my greatest moments were filled with love, laughter, and plenty of shenanigans with my best friend, my secret keeper, and confidant—my big brother Sam. Sam and I didn't have an easy life, albeit well provided for. However, growing up in a divorced home with a dysfunctional family life left us to depend upon each other emotionally. Sam and I both learned to bottle up our feelings and not make further waves in our home.

I was thirteen when I was first introduced to Jesus. I accepted Him so easily, but…and there is a "but" here…I asked Him into my heart almost daily. I was so scared of Jesus abandoning me and forsaking me that I would nearly beg Him to forgive my laundry list of thirteen-year-old sins on a pretty consistent basis. This wasn't because I was in a fear-based church; it was because my experience with abandonment and rejection was real. Oftentimes, I was never being heard or protected by my earthly father the way I needed—the way Sam and I both needed.

When I turned sixteen, I went to live with my mom, Sam left for college, and I rebelled. I became depressed and anxious. I battled an eating disorder and nearly died. Without the love and support of my mom, I wouldn't be here now to tell you my story.

Sam and I always remained close. Fortunately, I turned my life around at the age of twenty-two after I married and had my first child. I heard a powerful message from a missionary and I ran to the altar when he called us. It was like reuniting with a loving father, the Father I had forgotten.

MILITARY SPOUSE AND MOM OF 4

Although I had a life change, I continued to struggle with depression, panic attacks, and anxiety, often panicking about whether I would die from

Renee's brother, Sam Griffith

the attacks. So many hurts continued to follow me into adulthood. I settled into my role as a military spouse and mother of four children. I just went through the motions of life. I was much better at supporting others than myself and I truly thrived in seeing and pushing others to reach their goals and dreams.

My brother was an accomplished F-18 fighter pilot and consistently persevered through every goal he set. He was always a voice of reason for me when I was self-absorbed or needed encouragement. Sam knew how to make me laugh in moments I couldn't even find an ounce of good. He truly took on that role of a father figure to me on more than one occasion. He knew how to be stern with me, yet loving.

Sam was the kind of man who saw beyond one's flaws. He saw the good in everyone, even those who hurt him deeply. There are still moments I have trouble understanding that level of forgiveness he displayed to others. Always a source of optimism, he truly saw the bright side of everything and I didn't appreciate that until much later.

Sam wasn't perfect. I know he had internal struggles, but despite that, he still loved and cared for others in the best way possible. So when I got the call on December 14, 2011, that he had been killed in Afghanistan, I felt the breath leave my body. I thought I'd die from the pain. I was not prepared for such a moment. How could anyone be? My world and everything I knew changed in a second.

A FATEFUL SHIFT SWITCH

In an incredible act of bravery, my brother switched shifts with another Marine who had been under heavy fire the day before. The team of U.S. Marines and Royal Marines were ambushed and Sam exposed himself to gain a visual. A Taliban sniper shot and killed Sam instantly. Sam's actions saved his entire team and every one of them came home safely.

The following is an excerpt from the eulogy I wrote and spoke at his memorial service:

> Sam was not consumed with the lusts of this world. He lived a humble life. My brother has made me reevaluate my priorities. What impact do I want to make in this one life I've been given? You see, if his death doesn't change me, if it doesn't make me want to be a better person, a better Christian, if it doesn't make me want to pursue God with everything within me, then I will never have peace with his passing. I will always ask why.
>
> I stand here today, ready and willing to recommit myself to the cause for Christ. The Father says, "There is no greater love than to lay one's life down for his friends" (John 15:13). Sam was everybody's friend. God sent his one and only son, the King of Kings, to live as a pauper, a servant, with no title…to die for you and me. My brother left his family, his wife, and his sons. He willingly left his homeland, fought with everything he had, and laid his life down for you…and for me. What greater love is there? What other greater display of Christ is there than to live humbly as he did and die to save another?[1]

The irony of my words is that after the memorial was over, after the world moved on, after I realized I was just the sibling and of no significant value to the outside world where parents and widows are honored, I didn't know how to move forward. I struggled with PTSD, deep depression, and crushing anxiety. My memory lapsed and I argued with everyone I could. I was angry, I was in pain, and I was alone. How could I possibly take my own advice and pursue God the way I just told 1,800 people to do?

> What I know to be true about God is that He is near whether we feel Him close or not. This is why He gives us His Word to rely on, not our emotions. His Word is truth and if He says He is near to me, then He is, regardless of whether I can feel Him. His Word is His promise to me that, "Even when you cannot feel me close to you, I am close to you because my word says I am, and I cannot lie." Numbers 23:19 and Isaiah 41:10 helped me see this even more clearly. These are the times I had to rely on the Word of God, not my feelings.

---

1. Renee Nickell, *Always My Hero: The Road to Hope & Healing Following My Brother's Death in Afghanistan* (Pinehurst, TX: LifeWise Books, 2019).

The house was quiet. I began to think of my life and ask myself how I could find meaning in it again. My relationship with God was pushed aside like every other relationship in my life. Not that those around me didn't matter, but I felt *I* didn't matter. I walked out into the garage and I grabbed a bottle of wine out of the fridge. It was one that had been there for the previous six months since I don't drink wine that often. I returned to my bedroom, walked to the medicine cabinet, opened it and grabbed my bottle of Xanax. It was the bottle my doctor gave me the day Sam was killed. The bottle was only missing the one pill I took so I could sleep after the 48-hour drive to Dover.

That experience seemed like a dream now. I hated taking medication. I hated not feeling in control, but really, I wasn't in control anyway. I was so out of control. I sat on the side of the bed, lifted my feet off the cold hardwood floors, and placed them on the bed frame. I could feel the shape of the wood frame as my toes curled around its edges. I held a bottle of wine in one hand and a bottle of Xanax in the other as I contemplated taking my own life. I could just go to sleep. *How much of each would I have to take for all the pain to disappear?*

I do know that there was this fear inside of me that didn't want to take that risk, but I just didn't know how to make the pain stop. I just sat there staring at each of these bottles. I felt like my life was over and as I lay back, tears streamed down my face. I cried my eyes out, and wished someone knew how to help me. Wasn't there someone who would pull me out of this hole? Wasn't there someone who understands how much pain I was feeling? I just curled up in a fetal position, barely able to catch my breath.

The thoughts began to cross my mind of my husband and children finding me dead on the floor. *Did I want them to experience the pain of losing me? Did I want them to feel how I was feeling in that moment?* So many thoughts raced through my mind. *What would happen to their lives if I took my own? How would my mother cope with losing another child?* Honestly, I didn't think much of my other family. I had never really felt like I belonged to them anyway. Maybe they would be relieved. Maybe all along they had wished it were me that was dead and not Sam.

All of a sudden, there was a knock on the front door…[2]

---

2. Ibid.

THE HOLY SPIRIT INTERVENES

Even though the knock on the door was a close friend, I believe it was the Holy Spirit that prompted her to check on me. I also believe she saved my life that day. Do I believe it was a miracle? Absolutely!

Would I have taken those pills? I don't know. I'd like to think that no matter what, I would have thrown them down, called someone, and told them I needed help.

That isn't always the case. Those feelings cause us to feel shame. We don't want to burden others with our problems. Depression with PTSD is a lonely place. Thankfully, God intervened that day and I went into a treatment center.

The hard work had just begun. While I did a great job at managing my depression, the world around me was in a downward spiral. My relationships were failing, my teenage daughter was also dealing with PTSD and acting out. My marriage was on the fritz and we were fighting constantly. Grief was like a wave that just kept knocking me off my feet over and over again. Years went by in which I merely existed. Then I found Rex.

A HORSE HELPS IN HEALING

I was introduced to Rex on a beautiful day in the country. A ministry for veterans called Paws for Reflection in the small town of Midlothian, Texas, has licensed therapists who are trained in treating PTSD, particularly in combat veterans. While I have no experience with the difficulties combat veterans face, I do believe that military families who lose loved ones in war experience a significant amount of trauma.

I had no plan to get too close to Rex. His size alone terrified me. In the light, he appeared midnight in color and his height was intimidating. I focused back to Tristan and we got to know each other a bit, made a little small talk about my past and it seemed that very quickly our session was up. *Ok, I can start to see the appeal.* I felt comforted and safe being able to share with this soothing beauty of a gentle giant by my side.

I stood there and stared at Rex. My hands trembled with both shame and disappointment in myself as I began to approach Rex. In that moment, I was broken. I was real. I was honest. For the first time in a long time, I was able to acknowledge my brokenness. Rex turned towards me. He approached me and placed his head on my shoulder.

I leaned into him. I slowly raised the rope harness and place it around his head and tied it. I was now able to grab Rex by the reins. *I did it!* I was elated. I couldn't believe I just did that. I felt as if I had just conquered Mount Everest.

Session after session, I grew in confidence. Rex and I became good friends. He knew my deepest and darkest pain and he loved me more for it. He helped heal my marriage and my relationship with my daughter. He taught me things about myself I could never face alone. Rex, the big, scary horse I was terrified of, saved my life…and I am forever grateful.[3]

I can't speak highly enough about equine-assisted therapy in the treatment of PTSD. Our family has become very fond of horses since then. They are the most mysterious and kind animals I've ever experienced.

Though I learned many new things during horse therapy, I also knew it would still take time to shift the changes into our home. Callie (my therapist) had warned me, "Things will get worse before they get better." What she meant was when you begin to implement change in your home, there will be resistance because it is different from what the family has been doing for years. We were retraining ourselves how to be better parents, better communicators, better friends, etc. There was fear in moving forward…in a different direction than where we were previously headed. We had been headed for destruction, but God had a different plan for us.[4]

What happened in the following year after completing treatment was learning to face those dark places of my past, learning to forgive those who may not deserve my forgiveness, but doing it because it actually set me free. Jesus didn't die for us because we deserved it. He died for us to save us from hell. It's not easy to forgive, but I have found it to be the most impactful action I could do to set *me* free.

FINDING A PURPOSE

Not only did I have to start facing reality, I had to find purpose. The best way I found in my journey to find purpose was helping others. I decided it was time to write a book about my journey, praying it would help validate the pain

3. Ibid.
4. Ibid.

of others and offer them hope. It was a hard journey to relive the pain, but I knew there was greater purpose in it. I wouldn't have had the incredible opportunity to reach you, the reader, right now had I not written my story and taken a step of faith in my being transparent, honest, and raw.

Every year, my mom and step-dad hold an annual golf tournament that honors my brother Sam and our nation's heroes. We come together with members of the community and donate 100 percent of the proceeds to the Renewal Coalition.

The Renewal Coalition offers retreats to combat veterans and their families at no cost as a way to recon-

Renee Nickell holds a copy of her book, *Always My Hero: The Road to Hope & Healing Following My Brother's Death in Afghanistan.*

nect and reintegrate. We have been able to successfully donate more than six figures to this organization over the past seven years.

Sam's death changed me. It wrecked me and it almost destroyed me. I know I have a purpose. I also have the responsibility to use my life to help others and live it to the fullest in a way that honors the sacrifice of our heroes, especially my hero, Sam.

What I have had to learn through the pain and the heartache, through the trauma and the hard days...the days I wasn't sure I would make it, is that life didn't end the day Sam died. If it had, I'd be with him right now and so would everyone else who loved him. That's not how it works. We are left here to grieve, to work through the pain, so God can do a work in us and in others that would not happen otherwise.

I had to learn to live on purpose and with purpose...a kind of purpose I never had before. I was a wife, I was a mother, I was a daughter, but I did not know my purpose. Isn't that what we all are searching for?[5]

---

5. Ibid.

God loves me and He loves you. He cares about the deepest, darkest places of our souls and His desire is to walk with us through the valleys and over the mountaintops.

> There is something beautiful to be said about redemption. There is still redemption in the loss, regardless of whether we see it, when we see it, or if we even choose to see it. I remember praying to God after Sam's funeral that somehow, I could make a difference. I didn't know how. I didn't want to make a difference for my own benefit, but I wanted to know that somehow, someone's life was changed because of Sam's death. I prayed that someone would be affected in such a way that the trajectory of their life was changed.[6]

God has opened my eyes to beautiful blessings I could not see before. When I made the choice to walk through my healing, God opened a world to me I never dreamed possible. He wants to do that for you.

HELPFUL ORGANIZATIONS

Here are some organizations that assisted me in my recovery:

+ Paws for Reflection, equine-assisted therapy; www.pawsforreflection-ranch.org

+ Renewal Coalition, assisting wounded service members and their families; www.renewalcoalition.org

+ Tragedy Assistance Program for Survivors (TAPS); www.taps.org

—Renee Nickell

www.reneenickell.com

Facebook: @rmnickell

Instagram: @renee_nickell

Twitter: @rmnickell

---

6. Ibid.

★ 14 ★

JOHNATHAN STIDHAM

"Jesus Healed Me of PTSD"

My name is Johnathan Stidham and this is my story about how Jesus healed me of PTSD. After successfully completing a tour in Iraq in 2008, I returned home to marry my beautiful wife of now thirteen years at the church we grew up in. During this time, I knew that before my enlistment in the Marine Corps was over, I would deploy again, but I don't believe anyone in our unit was prepared to receive those orders to Afghanistan after only four months home from Iraq. So immediately after getting married, I had to return back to base for a company briefing on when we would officially leave and how long we would have to prepare for the deployment.

After a couple months of training there, we landed in the desert of Afghanistan. I still remember our battalion captain's speech to us before we headed out on our first mission. It was *the* Independence Day speech. It was highly motivating and left every man in that room wondering what the captain knew that we didn't...and what we were about to get ourselves into.

Johnathan Stidham served tours in
Iraq and Afghanistan.

NO AIR COVERAGE OR FOOD DROPS

The average day was around 115 to 120 degrees outside. Because of the nature of our mission, we were so far down south in Afghanistan that we couldn't get air coverage. This is horrible when you're in combat; we could not receive air drops of food for the first couple of months.

We became extremely creative in that situation. For instance, we would take a sock and put a bottle of water or beverage inside it, soak the sock in water, and leave it outside all night so we could wake up to a cold drink. Yes, someone in our group had passed science class. We were unable to shower during for a month or two and grew extremely tired of eating MREs (meals ready to eat) so we decided that we would start to buy sheep from the locals.

The entire deployment was one that could never be forgotten, from losing great men in combat to being in firefights where you didn't know if you were coming out alive.

REALITY HITS CLOSE TO HOME

For me, reality set in one day when rounds were being shot at us and landing no more than five feet away, in front of our feet. Something snapped as we dropped our guns and laughed until we cried because the rounds were not hitting us. Yes, it sounds crazy—because it was crazy. The pressure of war had taken its toll on our minds.

One evening, we decided to wake up and buy a sheep, build a fire during the day, and eat. We bought a sheep from the locals for five American dollars and had a feast. That night, we coiled up in a 360-degree fighting position with our vehicles outside the post because one of our vehicles had been attacked that day. That morning, we woke up to a disaster; we had slept on a bomb. When our vehicle went to move forward, the bomb that was connected to a pressure plate blew up, sending shrapnel one way and the concussion wave toward me and others standing around in the same vicinity.

After arriving back in the United States, I was sent over to the Wounded Warrior Battalion at Camp Lejeune, North Carolina, to continue recovering from the trauma I experienced while overseas. I spent the next year at inpatient and outpatient centers for PTSD. At one time, I was on over sixteen medications to help maintain some kind of a normal lifestyle. After a year of going back and forth with chronic headaches, I had radiofrequency ablation surgery on the back of my head to cauterize all of the nerves. As I was healing, I had a profound encounter with the Holy Spirit in which He told me I would do things in my life that the doctors said were impossible.

THE LORD OPENS DOORS

In 2012, I was officially retired from the United States Marine Corps as a wounded veteran with PTSD and other sustained injuries. With nearly two years of counseling after the deployment to Afghanistan, I felt like the bottom had dropped out from under my feet. I thought, *Where am I going to go? What am I going to do now?*

My wife and I moved home and became very active in our church and community. Out of nowhere, the Lord began to open up opportunities for me to travel and preach. Once when I was preaching in Mississippi, the Spirit of the Lord began to move. Suddenly, miracles started to happen. Deaf ears were opened. Then a guy who came in a wheelchair got up and started running around the building, screaming, "I get to go back to Africa!" He had been a missionary in Africa and was injured there, suffering a herniated disc when the vehicle he was riding in hit a bad bump. Eventually, this prohibited him from walking without severe pain. But he was now healed.

GOD: WILL YOU GO WHERE I SEND YOU?

That night, I went back to my hotel room and experienced one of the worst headaches I ever had. I had watched God perform miracles, yet *I* was still in pain, feeling broken and on medications because of PTSD. That night, I remember getting so upset with God that I yelled out to Him. His reply changed me forever. He said, "John, if I never heal you, will you still go where I send you and pray for miracles in the lives of those who are there?" In tears, I cried back, "Yes I will."

Weeks went by after that encounter with the Lord. One Sunday morning, I was with my family worshiping at our home church, when I felt someone come and lay their hand upon my head.

HIT BY A HEALING FIRE

Fire ran from the top of my head all the way to my feet and I collapsed to the floor under the fire of God. When I got back up, there was no one there, so I started asking if anyone had seen someone lay their hands on me. No one had seen anyone beside me; they only saw me fall under the power of God.

As I left that service, I could feel the change in my body. I was thinking clearly, my back was pain-free, and there were other noticeable differences as well. Weeks went by and I had no headaches, no nightmares, and no panic attacks or anxiety. God had touched me in a very extraordinary way. During

Johnathan Stidham

that time, I came off all of the medications and had no side effects from doing so. (A note of caution: please do not stop your medications without your doctor's supervision.)

I share my story today, years after that encounter with the Lord, having spoken to so many in the military who have asked me how in the world I have reached this point. I am so much at peace and doing all of things I enjoy, like traveling the world, owning a business, planting churches, and spending time with my family. I always say, "Jesus touched me!" I was healed of PTSD, not from my experiences, but from my experiences owning me. If He did it for me, He can do it for you, too!

—Johnathan Stidham

AUSTON O'NEILL

National Bugler for Spirit of '45

Although Auston O'Neill is not a veteran, he has a heart for all who have served our country.

A medical condition disqualified Auston when he tried to enlist many years ago, but he has dedicated his retirement years to making sure our servicemen and women receive the honors they deserve.

At age seventy-two, Auston and his wife, Bonnie, travel the country so he can play "Taps" for veterans at their funerals or on special occasions, such as Memorial Day and Spirit of '45 Day. The mournful tune, the last call played at U.S. military bases in the evening, is traditionally played by a lone bugler or trumpeter at funerals, memorial services, and wreath-laying ceremonies.

Auston O'Neill plays "Taps" at Arlington National Cemetery.

Auston is the national bugler for Spirit of '45, a group of organizations and individuals working to preserve and honor the legacy of the men and women of America's World War II generation. Spirit of '45 Day is observed throughout America each year on the second weekend in August.

His father, Auston Sr., was a decorated combat infantryman during World War II, having served in New Guinea in the Pacific Theater. However, no bugler or trumpeter played "Taps" at his funeral. Instead, the tune was played on a boom box. "I thought it was a travesty," Auston says.

Not long afterward, Auston found out about Bugles Across America, a nationwide network of buglers who are available to play "Taps" at veterans' funerals. So he signed up.

Auston's played "Taps" through heavy downpours, thunder, and lightening. He's played in 4-degree temperatures that froze his lips to his mouthpiece. Then he was recruited to be the national bugler for Spirit of '45.

"I'm doing this to honor my dad, but I'm also doing this to honor all the World War II veterans who died to make this country as it is today," Auston says. "We wouldn't have the freedoms that we have if those men and women hadn't served and died."

DEALING WITH TERMINAL CANCER

Amazingly, he's done all of this while dealing with terminal cancer that spread to his lymph nodes.

"You know, I believe in God for my healing," Auston says. "I'm getting stronger as the days go by. I'm not getting weaker."

On their Facebook page for Auston's birthday on January 28, 2020, Bonnie wrote that he doesn't look his age "because God has blessed him.... There has always been three in our marriage. My husband, myself, and God our Father. That is the only reason we have been able to experience this journey together for almost forty-six years."

God is limitless and His Word is true. He is ever ready to heal us if we only will believe.

For more about the Spirit of '45, visit:

www.facebook.com/Spirito45UnityTour
www.spiritof45.org

For more about Bugles Across America, visit:

www.buglesacrossamerica.org

PART 3:
HEALING

★ 16 ★
STEPS TO HEALING

Through the years, I have learned how strong trauma is and the effects it can have on your life. I want to get rid of any power of the enemy, especially where trauma is concerned. Trauma enters your body like an earthquake and causes everything inside you to shift—and not in a good way.

After a period of time, stress comes into the picture. Stress hormones destroy the immune system, which is why we get so many prayer requests for autoimmune deficiency diseases.

You need to keep your immune system healthy because whether you're going to the store or flying somewhere, you're exposed to many kinds of disease-causing bacteria. There is no way you can keep a physical protective screen between you and others. When trauma comes in, it not only affects every cell in your body, it will remain with you until you die in the natural.

God is going to take out and clean up every single problem cell with a Holy Ghost scalpel and remove every bit of trauma in your traumatized body.

STEP 1: REALIZE THE PROBLEM
Identification Is Key

When you have a physical illness, you go to a medical doctor. Once your problem is identified, treatment options are discussed. Medications may take care of the issue temporarily or surgery may be advised to simply remove the problem. Recovery may require a change of activity or diet. Rehabilitation may include special exercises, supervised activity, or lifestyle changes. Occasionally, optimal healing may require a change in environment or climate. You may have to compromise for the best possible outcome.

This book can apply the same treatment pattern to your spiritual life. You have to realize you have a problem, recognize its cause, determine who can help you, submit to the required treatment, recover, rehabilitate, and then reach out to help others.

Ask Yourself...

Symptoms of a spiritual heart disease may be more difficult to see outwardly, but they can be identified by answering some questions:

> Do you feel trapped? Is there something preventing you from living the life you long for? Is someone or something preventing you from reaching your dream? Do you believe someone is blocking your way? Are previous events affecting your life today?

> How do you view the barrier in front of you? Is it large or small? Can you hop over it or do you need a ladder or bulldozer? Is the barrier positive or negative? A barrier or wall around yourself can both prevent you from progress and protect you from danger.

> Who built the wall? Did someone build the wall of fear around you or did you build it to prevent anyone from getting into your space?

> Can you see through or over the wall? Those people on the other side are happy and laughing, surrounded by healthy, active friends and family. Do you remember days like that from years ago and long to join the joyful crowd?

> Do you feel trapped by fear and loneliness? Do you feel you have no strength or courage to take that first step? Does taking a breath sometimes exhaust you? Do you cry easily and withdraw to the safety of isolation?

Your pain may seem to be in your mind, causing frequent headaches. Holding your body tightly may cause added muscle aches or joint pain. Nervousness or chest pain may overwhelm you at times. Your stomach may feel like it's in knots and frequent bathroom breaks don't help.

Resentment, anger, frustration, shame, bitterness, fear—so many descriptive words can apply to anyone with a broken or damaged heart. To protect and prevent further injury, each person develops a way to avoid the cause or find an outlet to recovery. This book will lead you not only to healing but also to victorious recovery.

If you answered "yes" to any of those questions, your heart has been damaged and you need help. I am not sending you to a medical doctor. You need to visit the Great Physician to get healed. God has the answers. His Word is medicine and He is the Surgeon who can cut out the bad stuff that has cluttered up your life.

Recognize the Cause

Let's look back for just a few minutes. Do you remember the list I asked you to complete earlier in this book? Look at it again. Do you remember an incident or trauma from years ago that caused or started your pain? Allow the Holy Spirit to show you what happened as if you were the observer, not the victim.

Was there a particular incident, such as a death in the family, a devastating car accident, the loss of a friend, a physical injury, service during conflict, or physical, mental, or sexual abuse? Often, the hurt may seem small in one person's eyes, but in yours, it was monumental. Since that stressful traumatic event, memories may pop up at strange times and affect many areas of your life, even giving you nightmares at night.

Life happens, yes, but recovering from such an incident doesn't happen overnight. Physical injuries can heal, grief after a death can eventually fade, and a pattern of abuse may end, but PTSD can repeat itself for years. Certain aspects need to be identified and dealt with through proper ministry to gain freedom from this form of bondage.

Believing a lie is often the first step toward isolation. For instance, someone calls you an ugly name and another person repeats it or calls you something worse. You don't know how to respond. You don't feel ugly or bad, but two people say you are, so there must be some truth to it, right? The next day, they say more hurtful things to you.

The actual words could have been harmless, but the tone of voice or the look they gave you seemed vicious and mean. You were hurt physically or mentally. Even if that person apologized later or came back again with kindness or love, the memory of the bad experience remains.

You Did Nothing Wrong

Something irritated a person and made them mad. Their anger was turned on the first person they saw: you! You hadn't done or said anything, but you got the brunt of their outburst again. Blame attached itself to you and you accepted it. You felt you did something wrong and deserved the angry retribution. But that's a lie. You did nothing to cause the situation.

An injured animal tends to hide from danger. A child or abused person does the same thing. It is called isolation—staying away from potential harm. If incidents happen with several different people, such as a bullied child might experience on a playground, avoiding people in general may become the norm.

Challenged people have a very difficult time in this area. A speech impediment, a defective arm or leg, the absence of a limb, or any abnormality can bring ridicule. Adults with a disability may receive strange looks and hurtful comments. Slow learners or those who learn differently are labeled *dumb* when many are actually brilliant. Some people are just cruel and will find some way to make fun of others.

If a person doesn't learn to positively release powerful emotions, the destructive nature of angry words will pass from one to another, causing more pain. The larger or stronger person passes their pain down to the next available or safe person, who then strikes out at the next. A bully won't go after a father or teacher, but he will pick on a younger, smaller, helpless child. That child may take his pain and frustrations out on something smaller, even their beloved dog or cat.

Have you ever watched or listened to a small child with their toys? Children repeat what they hear and see; they will express love or anger, depending on what they've experienced. A young girl who's been spanked will punish her dolls. A young boy will get violent with his toy weapons or action figures. They are merely repeating what they have learned. If the child has misbehaved and needs correction, proper parenting would be to explain what was expected of them, not become abusive.

Taking our anger or frustrations out on innocent people makes them believe the lie that they're somehow to blame. An upsetting phone call, a rude driver in traffic, an unmet expectation—so many things can upset our plans. Instead of a healthy outlet, the frustration becomes destructive to anyone or anything in our path.

"It's all your fault!" can do so much damage to a person who doesn't understand the situation. Confusion enters and they wonder, *What did I do to cause this?* Without explanation, confusion turns to fear of the next uncontrolled outburst of temper or violence.

Whatever the lie, the first brick of that wall was laid. With each episode, another brick is placed.

If you are hurting right now, do you really want to pass your pain on to your spouse, your children, or your friends? Make a quality decision to stop the pain in your life so you don't become the cause of another's pain.

Determine Your Triggers

When PTSD is a problem, there are triggers that often bring back memories that can cause the person to relive the same traumatic pain again and again. For example, if a teenager has been sexually abused by her father, any male who comes near her wearing his cologne or aftershave will trigger her fear. She'll feel trapped. She is also susceptible to further attacks or injury because of her fear/freeze reaction. The mere whiff of that cologne is a serious trigger in this young lady's life.

What sends you, your friend, or family member off into fits of rage or cowering in fear? It can be a word, how someone talks or walks, or a noise. Just seeing a person or talking about the person who caused you pain can trigger a serious physiological, physical, and emotional reaction.

Identify and be aware of your personal triggers. Stay away from them. Communicate with your close friends or family. They should know they aren't the direct cause of your outbursts.

Unmet Expectations

Don't expect other people to solve your problem, take away your painful memories, or meet your unrealistic expectations. You can seek help from pastors, counselors, or medical professionals, but your family or friends will probably not have the answers you need, so don't expect them.

Expecting too much from your children or using abusive words to try to control them can have lifelong effects on them. They will feel they are never *good enough*. Your negative behavior can be learned and practiced by the ones you have affected. It is a spiritual principle, a generational curse.

When a couple gets a divorce, unless a very patient, consistent explanation is given, the children will often blame themselves. They believe a lie— that the fighting, yelling, and abuse is their fault. Claiming this blame can also start codependent behavior.

If a mother dies while giving birth, her child, when older, may often feel responsible. Careful explanation and love must be offered to stop this lie from taking root and growing into a huge problem.

A bride believes her groom is "just like my kind, gentle, loving father," but discovers her new husband has a mean lazy streak when he is tired and overworked. Expectations of a fun, perfect home go out the window with every angry tirade. His self-control is gone. Making a good impression on her is unnecessary once the vows have been said. In turn, the young husband can be dismayed when he finds his bride redoing his chores, sulking, wearing face cream, or snoring.

Did your Dad want you to become a doctor, but you hate hospital smells? Does your spouse expect you to maintain a fulltime job when you'd rather stay home to care for and homeschool your precious children?

Unmet expectations are often at the root of disagreement and conflict. Discussing those expectations can sometimes resolve the differences, but many people just get irritated and turn away. If you don't spell out exactly what you expect from another, don't question why they don't do what you expect them to do. No one can read your mind.

Broken promises, shattered confidences, destroyed beliefs, crushed dreams, financial ruin, natural disaster, failing health, fragmented relationships, a dysfunctional family—all seem to be insurmountable when staring you in the face. You feel you have to do your own fighting, win your own battles, and protect yourself any way you can. Stress explodes and trauma penetrates the heart.

Perhaps a friend said something to hurt you. A parent degraded you instead of surrounding you with loving encouragement. A look of hate or anger struck your heart. After a few more negative words or actions, your self-esteem was knocked right out from under you.

A Wall Around Your Heart

As you add another brick for every negative comment, look, or thought, isolation comes quickly. You are building a wall around your heart. Each hurtful jab from another is like a little arrow that pierces you. The pain is not easy to manage, so you add another brick.

However, healing those wounds can be easy. Your protection from further damage is love—love like you have never experienced before. It will pour out of you to overflow others who are also trapped.

You may hear the comment, "God is teaching you something." Please understand, God gives *good* things, not bad things. *He loves you.* He gave life to you. He gives you every breath and every heartbeat. He didn't create you to punish you with calamity or pain! Indeed, He is the One who can take that pain away and heal you completely.

The Enemy Fights On

If bad things don't come from God, where do they come from? Throughout the Bible, you read about opposing spiritual forces. There is good (God) and evil (Satan). God created man to live in a peaceful, rewarding relationship with Him for eternity. Satan rebelled and was thrown out of heaven. His warped, twisted mind is still fighting the battle to become a god himself. He will do whatever he can to separate God from His creation, His children.

From Genesis through Revelation, you can see God's love saving His people from the enemy's hate and anger. A simple belief in Jesus Christ as the Savior of the world gives the Christian free entrance into an eternity of peace with God in heaven.

No, every bad thing doesn't mean Satan is everywhere causing trouble for everyone. Man's evil nature comes up with some of the trouble all by itself. But Satan has many fallen angels who can speak wicked suggestions into man's ear. It is up to man to judge those thoughts against God's Word and make the choice to follow God or give in to evil ideas.

You will learn about spirits that are allowed entry into a life through sin. They have to be addressed and removed from a person. Some have been passed down through the bloodline generation after generation. When the affected person is cooperative and willing to accept a change, they can escape that prison. A knowledgeable Christian can break those ties and cut that connection from previous generations.

Are You Ready to Be Free?

God is Love. He doesn't pour calamity all over you to teach you any lessons. He may allow some stress into your life at times. Just as a child must learn how to handle a hot stove or a sharp object, you have to know how to handle life's ups and downs. Your best education is from experience, not reading a book or listening to another.

The Bible has endless lessons and examples to learn from. You can find the answers you need within God's Word—and I trust you will. You may see something different every time you read certain parts of the Bible, depending on what you need at the time and what God wants to tell you. His Word is truly amazing.

STEP 2: REPENT

Accept God by Faith

To access God's life and love, you do have to accept Him by faith. In simple terms, you must be saved. This is not difficult. You do not have to run to the church or the altar to find Him. Right where you are at this moment is the right place for you.

God is your Father. He is always with you and will never leave you. Jesus, God's only Son, died for your sins long ago, so you have the right and privilege to be adopted into His family. Jesus paid the ultimate price and paved the way for you.

God will never force you to do anything. He will always allow you free choice. Choosing to sin, or doing something wrong, will always separate you from Him. Repentance, asking for His forgiveness, will restore your fellowship and intimacy with your heavenly Father.

If you disobey your earthly father or another authority, you have to make it right by apologizing or incurring some penalty. If you follow the rules, peace is maintained. The same principle applies to your relationship with God. If you follow God's Word, the Bible, your intimacy with Him is intact. If you break His laws and go against His Word, your penalty is spiritual separation from Him.

He Will Never Leave...But You Might

God will never leave you or forsake you, but you may not hear from Him or be protected in the same way. When you shut the door in His face and break the communication connection, He didn't cut you off. *You* separated yourself from Him.

Ask for forgiveness for the things you have done wrong in the past and welcome Jesus to enter your heart and stay there. He can and will live within you when you are a true believer. His Holy Spirit enters your heart and is always available for instant advice and conversation whenever you need Him. He may even talk to you before you ask for help. That's part of His assignment from God.

To repent means you ask for forgiveness and then change the direction of your life. If someone hurts you, apologizes, and then continues to hurt you in the same way, that apology was worthless and insincere. One can't apologize for wrongdoing and continue to do it. Becoming a Christian and following

God's Word brings a sincere and total change in a person's life. True repentance brings God's total forgiveness for a sincerely changed person.

After repentance and with God's help, you will make good choices based on the direction in His Word. You will step onto the path God has planned for you.

Just Talk to God

Communicating with God is not difficult. Praying is simply talking to God. No fancy words are necessary and you don't need any particular place or time. Use words you understand. The most common prayer, I believe, is simply, "Father, help!"

If you need more guidance, try this prayer:

Father, I know I haven't always made the right choices or said the right words. Please forgive me. I need Your help. Please, Jesus, come into my heart right now and guide my thoughts, actions, and footsteps. I want to walk in Your perfect will for my life. Open my mind and heart as I read this book. Show me what I need to do to live in Your freedom and love. In Jesus's name. Amen.

Realize this: God does not forgive sin. He hates sin with an everlasting passion. He forgives *you*, the sinner. He forgives you for making a wrong choice in that situation. He loves you and wants to guide you to make the correct choice next time. Pay attention to Him and obey what He says.

There are also sins of omission. Certainly, you remember not doing what your parent told you to do at least once during your youth. Mom told you to do the dishes and you left the house to play with your friends instead. Dad told you to get gas and clean the car after using it on Friday night. You left the car running on fumes and messy with trash. Nothing was hurt or broken; you just didn't follow orders. You didn't obey.

Obedience Is Wisdom and Faith

To some, obedience is a bad word. They believe it means a form of slavery, to do what you are told without question. But obedience is wisdom and faith.

God has His instructions clearly written in His Word. A person may think they are good because they have obeyed the Ten Commandments their entire life, but the Bible contains other rules—rules, not suggestions. There is a lot more instruction and explanation throughout the sixty-six books of God's Bible.

Most people are guilty of the sin of omission just as much as those sins they choose to commit. What has God told you lately? Be aware that He will ask you to do some things you may not want to do, like forgiving those who have hurt you. This is not easy or fun, but it's necessary for your well-being and healing.

STEP 3: FORGIVE...

Some Hurts Were Unintentional

Total recovery is often dependent on forgiveness. Yes, you ask God to forgive you. However, you will have to forgive those who hurt you, too. Some of those scars may have been inflicted intentionally, but many times, they were caused more by your perception of an incident.

If a man has a very bad day at work or a rough drive home through horrible traffic, his anger can easily be transferred to an unsuspecting spouse or child. After this occurs a few times, that behavior becomes expected "when Daddy comes home." Small children can assume they did something wrong and hide or withdraw.

Anger may be expressed physically by smashing in a door or breaking something. An accidental blow on another person can have long-lasting effects that may never totally heal. Severe punishment for disobedience, whether an isolated incident or repeated instances, can affect the body, mind, and spirit.

Your heart could have been injured because of someone else's sin, not yours. This is apparent when the sins of your ancestors are credited down the bloodline. (See Exodus 34:7.)

Rejection, shame, pain, hate—the list is long. All have their basis in fear and will rapidly add bricks to that protective wall if you allow it.

Your Unforgiveness Hurts You

The person who sinned against you isn't hurt when you don't forgive them. Instead, unforgiveness holds *you* captive and destroys your life. They don't deserve your forgiveness just like you didn't deserve God's forgiveness. Getting free is a choice to obey God's Word.

From the cross at Calvary, Jesus cried, *"Father, forgive them, for they do not know what they do"* (Luke 23:34).

Jesus taught us, *"Do not judge others, and you will not be judged. Do not condemn others, or it will all come back against you. Forgive others, and you will be forgiven"* (Luke 6:37 NLT).

Just as God forgives you for committing a sin, you must forgive the person who hurt you. You are not forgiving what they did to you; you are forgiving their wrong choice. You take that sin, place it on the cross, and leave it there.

What if they come back and hurt you again? Some believe Christians are weak because they don't fight back. But it takes a strong person to follow Jesus's instructions and example.

> *Then Peter came to Him and said, "Lord, how often shall my brother sin against me, and I forgive him? Up to seven times?" Jesus said to him, "I do not say to you, up to seven times, but up to seventy times seven."*
>
> (Matthew 18:21–22)

> *If you forgive those who sin against you, your heavenly Father will forgive you. But if you refuse to forgive others, your Father will not forgive your sins.* (Matthew 6:14–15 NLT)

> *Then the angry king sent the man to prison to be tortured until he had paid his entire debt. That's what my heavenly Father will do to you if you refuse to forgive your brothers and sisters from your heart.*
>
> (Matthew 18:34–35 NLT)

They Will Answer to God

Your prayer and your forgiveness do not release the person who has wronged you from answering to God for their actions. God says, *"Vengeance is Mine"* (Romans 12:19). He will deal with that person and their heart for what they did to you. There is little that you can do to get back at anyone. God, on the other hand, knows them well and can reach them where they can't hide or run away.

Forgiveness is part of God's nature. He forgives you numerous times a day. Christians must learn to walk in forgiveness all along their journey. Part of your recovery is to learn this important and difficult lesson. Make sure you have confessed all sin to the Father and forgive others so you can be forgiven.

There is no sin so horrible that God cannot forgive you. He knows all of your actions, words, and thoughts from your first breath of life to your last. If He can forgive the men who killed His only Son, He can forgive you. Don't ever say you can't forgive yourself. You do not have that power. Forgiveness comes from God, not you. Accept His forgiveness and be healed.

STEP 4: RECOVER

Make Better Choices

Make a quality decision to make better choices. Seek God and His Holy Spirit for their wisdom in every situation. He is in control and can guide you down the best path designed specifically for you.

Find the areas of stress in your life and release it. Again, ask for God's guidance. Take every area and lay it at the cross. Trust that He will take care of the situation.

Break Down Those Walls

You are the one who built the wall around you. Most start their own wall at a young age. Whether someone called you a name or told a lie about you, something hurt you. Mental and spiritual hurts are usually buried within the mind and heart.

Physical hurts usually heal over quickly and are forgotten. However, in the case of abuse, physical pain can become so intertwined with the mental pain that it is difficult to distinguish between them. Frequent punishment, whether warranted or not, can breed resentment, anger, and violence. The victim's age makes no difference. Child, spousal, and elder abuse are too common in today's world.

Your parents, your spouse, your friends, and your family are not responsible for your happiness. Parents are given the responsibility to train a child in the way they should go, but the Bible doesn't tell parents to keep their offspring smiling and happy. A spouse cannot make you happy 24/7 either. They can love and care for you, but the Bible doesn't say anything about keeping the other joyful. Same thing with friends.

Are you experiencing survival stress or survivor's guilt? If you were with a friend when they were killed in battle, or survived a car accident that left another dead, you may feel guilty that they died instead of you.

Instead of wanting to take that person's place, thank God that you are still alive to help others. God is in control and has kept you alive for His purpose. Shake off that stress or guilt and keep walking forward into your destiny.

Each person has an appointed time to join the Father in heaven. Your time has not arrived yet.

Joy Comes from God

True inner joy comes only from God. "The joy of the Lord is my strength"—how often did we sing those words as children! Happiness comes from within. You can choose to be happy because your heavenly Father is your Source of joy. Man cannot take that away from you. Yes, man can say and do hurtful things, but you have a choice to be offended or shake it off.

A child has a hard time setting boundaries with an abusive parent. However, after a certain age, everyone has the right and privilege of saying, "Thus far and no farther." In the natural, you may be saying that to a friend, partner, or parent; however, in reality, you are drawing the line in the sand for the enemy.

Satan uses people closest to you to undermine your self-esteem, your perfectly laid plans, your happiness, and your life. Seeds of jealousy, anger, frustration, or resentment can be planted and allowed to grow. Suddenly, a promotion, a bountiful garden harvest, or successful book launch has you on a cloud of happiness. Then someone says something to try to burst your bubble: "You're going to be working sixty hours a week." "I bet it's all zucchini!" "Who's going to buy *that?*"

Don't give another person the power to destroy you or your dreams. No one should have that much control of your life. God has the playbook and only sends good things to surround you. Everyone comes from their own experiences in life. Others are not going to see everything the same way you see it. Don't expect them to. God has them on their own path to their future.

Seek Wise Counsel

Asking advice from another is fine as long as you use wisdom in choosing the person. Advice on writing a book shouldn't come from a child or uneducated person. Discussing spiritual matters with an atheist is a waste of time. Seek counsel from a person who knows something about your situation.

You don't ask a plumber to cut your hair or a real estate agent to repair your car. Find someone with the expertise you need for the task at hand. Learn from someone who knows more than you. Once you have researched the subject using books, tapes, the Internet, a library, and other people, then you can make an informed decision as to the best path to take. Don't neglect God in your research. His advice is always the best.

Challenges Will Come

God *will* send challenging situations your way *for your own good* even though you may not realize it or want to accept it at the time. Think about a child or young person who is still in a *training* stage of life. If nothing different is introduced to them, they will not develop or learn. They will not become a mature adult. I'm sure you have encountered an older person who still acts like a child. It's possible they were totally sheltered and isolated from society, and thus never learned the necessary life lessons to succeed. The same principle is true with someone from another country. They do not understand the accepted customs or laws of this country.

Increasingly difficult experiences are placed before a young child, an adolescent, a teen-ager, and a young adult. Indeed, we never stop learning new things and each task may be more challenging than the last. These challenges are an important part of life. Some assignments may not be pleasant, but they help our physical, mental, and spiritual growth.

If you were hurt by a parent, does that mean all parents are mean and ugly? No. If a classmate made fun of your freckles or glasses, does that mean all classmates will reject you? No.

It is difficult to gloss over hurtful experiences thrown at you by those you love and respect, but you always have a choice to accept or reject their words or actions. One of my favorite thoughts is, *They don't know any better!*

On the cross, Jesus said the same thing regarding His enemies: *"Father, forgive them, for they do not know what they do"* (Luke 23:34).

Arguing or trying to convince another to change their mind can sometimes help, but often, you need to save your breath and energy. If someone is not open to listen to another side of the story, an argument will not change their opinion. Everyone comes from unique experiences and their deeply ingrained beliefs are difficult, if not impossible, to uproot.

Use Wisdom, Not Judgment

Maturity means you will use godly wisdom to correctly assess a situation and recognize what is truth and what is a lie. The men who killed Jesus were believing lies. They were told Jesus was evil, a traitor, and a heretic who was causing dissension in the temple and among the people of Israel. They acted on the lies because they couldn't recognize Truth when He was standing in front of them.

The Bible tells us not to judge people, but you *should* pay attention to their behavior. Do their words and actions line up with the Word of God and His love? Hurtful actions, hateful words, and lies come from the enemy, Satan. Love and truth come from God. Which are you going to choose?

You can live in truth and obedience to God's Word or live in the enemy's lies, where confusion, hate, and anger thrive.

If a certain thought goes through your mind and you wonder where it came from, ask yourself, "Does that sound like God? Does it line up with His Word and His purpose?" God will always tell you to do or say something that is best for you or another. For instance, if God tells you to talk to someone about Jesus, He usually has already softened their heart to listen. If it is simply your determination to get them saved, you may have a long battle that can chase them further away. Listen to what God is saying to you, then obey.

God May Give a Word of Warning

God's voice may also warn you as a means of protection. Pay attention. You may come close to a person or enter a room and feel very uneasy. God could be telling you to turn the other direction. This is particularly important if you are alone. Two or more people can pray for protection around each other. Listen and feel. You need His protection and instruction about what to do in every situation.

You can draw boundaries for people who may try to hurt you. First of all, you can leave their presence. No one will keep you there to be abused. You don't have to listen. Leave.

Avoiding your spouse or parent may not be so easy. Hurtful words or anger can escalate into heated arguments. You can and should excuse yourself and separate yourself until tempers fade. If someone won't discuss issues calmly, you may need to find a mediator, someone who can keep the situation under control.

Unfortunately, some people simply like to irritate others with unpleasant comments or embarrassing actions to start an argument. Again, you can excuse yourself from the situation and leave. If you choose to stay and engage, expect pain, anger, or tears.

To recover, you must control your environment and avoid bad situations. Get your strength back. Don't allow the negative to camp in your space. It will rear its ugly head because Satan's job is to try to destroy you. It is your choice to listen to him and his endless lies or rebuke him in Jesus's name.

To remedy depression, read all of the great positive Scripture verses you can find in His Word. Watch all of the funny TV shows or movies you can. Choose to be around uplifting people who will encourage you in your recovery.

If you fracture your leg, you will not be sitting or lying down with it in the air forever. Once the doctor says it's time, you will have physical therapy and exercise that leg routinely until full strength returns. The same goes for your wounded pride or hurt feelings. You can go to the Great Physician, take your medication (His Word), and start exercising your faith that the best is yet to come.

True Friends Will Lift You Up

If your old friends start dragging you backwards, find some new friends who will push you upwards. Jealous friends will drag you down. True friends will help you to be the best you can be. As you encourage one another, you will rejoice together all the way to the throne room to worship the One who brought you together.

"All things work together for good to those who love God" (Romans 8:28). That means *all* things. If you had not gone through some bad things, you couldn't help the next person get through their issues. Every action has bad and good aspects, just like life. I know you want to experience only the good and never the bad, but if you don't have a little bump in the road occasionally, you will never appreciate smooth sailing.

Plan well. Aim at your goal. Seek the experts who can help you recover, grow, and develop into the mature person God has destined you to become. God said, *"Do not touch my chosen people, and do not hurt my prophets"* (Psalm 105:15 NLT). If you are saved and one of God's children, you have an Advocate with the Father. Jesus is fighting for you before the throne of Almighty God. He knows what you are going through and what you are feeling. Jesus is your *best friend forever* and is available at all times. Your earthly friends and family may be scattered across the world, but Jesus is always with you.

Small children tell bullies, "My father will get you!" or "My big brother will fight you!" Guess what? That child is so right. Tell your tormentor the same thing. Your heavenly Father will take care of them in ways you couldn't even dream of. Your big brother, Jesus, will fight your battle for you while you stand by and watch.

Years ago, while going through a particularly difficult situation, a friend heard a short song that imbedded itself within her. When words were lost and nothing could console her, these words became her answer: "Glory, Jesus, glory, You do the fighting for me! Praise You, Jesus, praise You, in You there is always victory!" In stressful situations, my friend still remembers where true peace and ultimate victory is found.

Step into your God-appointed anointing. Step into His family and let Him take care of you and all of your problems. He is arranging all the details. Just thank Him and worship Him for His goodness, grace, mercy, and love. Thank Him for everything. Without Him, you truly are nothing, but with Him, you are everything.

Choose the joy of the Lord for it is your strength. (See Nehemiah 8:10.)

STEP 5: REHABILITATE

Reconnect Your Scattered Heart

Love is truly a choice. God is love, pure love. Jesus was the earthly embodiment of His Father's love. He loved when the normal human heart would have hated. Could you maintain love for the person beating you with a cat-o'-nine-tails shredding your flesh from your bones? Would you be able to show grace and mercy for the crowd yelling, "Crucify Him"?

I personally don't know anyone except Jesus who could maintain perfect love in those situations. He knew His calling, His purpose, and His assignment, and held out until the end.

Thinking back on my own life, I don't remember anyone in my early years who taught me how to protect my heart. I learned how to cross the street and use a knife safely, but who taught me to protect my spirit or my heart?

Who spoke to your heart to protect it from damage? There are plenty of books and information about what foods you should eat or exercises you can do to strengthen and keep your heart physically healthy. But where do you learn spiritual healing? Who gently collects the parts of a broken, shattered heart and puts it back together to beat stronger than ever? Only a healed and properly functioning heart can truly allow Jesus's love to flow through it to others.

Without that healing years ago, I couldn't minister to the hurting people I reach today. I would not feel their pain with Jesus's compassion or love. Words and details are not necessary. I often touch them and tears start to flow. Jesus's heart within me draws their pain right out of them.

Take Back the Parts of Your Heart

Through the years, you gave a little piece of your heart to many others. Think about it for a minute. Your parents, of course, were the first ones you trusted. Perhaps you loved siblings, a best friend, a teacher, or a mentor. Your first childhood crush was so cute. Your heart beat faster each time you even looked at them. Your first date, your first kiss…you willingly gave each one a piece of your heart.

With each person you meet, you make a choice. Will this person be allowed to affect you positively or negatively? When you are with them, do they make you feel good or bad? Do you feel love or hate? Peace or fear? Do you want to be with them or do you want to get away as soon as possible? Are they dragging you down or building you up?

Even thoughts of those people can stir up emotions. Thinking about your spouse should bring feelings of love and peace while dwelling on a lost love or abusive parent can cause nervousness and fear to overwhelm you.

Can you see how your heart can be divided into numerous pieces as love is felt and shared with another? Life goes on. You fall in love and give more pieces of your heart away. It happens numerous times before marriage is ever discussed. All are learning experiences before *the one* comes into view.

If your marriage ends in divorce, part of your heart walks out of your life. The word *heartbroken* is used to describe the emptiness and pain left behind. The medical community has even proven that calamity and destructive experiences can shred the heart muscle.

WHO'S TO BLAME?

Who was responsible for your broken heart? Who didn't meet your expectations?

Many people blame God for their failures. Maybe they believed God would give them a beautiful life no matter what they did or didn't do. A loved one died or a business was lost to bankruptcy. They worked hard and did their best, but they never tithed on their business profits, worshipped, or thanked God for their successful years.

They blamed other people or situations, but eventually turned their anger toward God. It was definitely God's fault, not theirs. They didn't think listening to God's voice of wisdom in business affairs was necessary. In the end, they blamed God.

They once loved God and willingly trusted Him with their heart. With the unfortunate events and disappointments of life, they withdrew that love, that faith, and their heart from God. Instead of drawing closer to the Source of all love and healing, they listened to the lies of the enemy and wandered the other direction. After a period of time, little by little, they take pieces of their heart back from those they once loved and their heart is hardened toward God. Their trust is gone, their faith is misplaced, and their heart shrivels into an unfeeling group of muscular tissues in their chest.

SATAN WANTS HARD HEARTS

Outwardly, their face becomes wrinkled, eyes lose their sparkle, posture shrinks, shoulders fall, voices weaken, and the person looks years older than they are. Diseases attach themselves to damaged body parts because the enemy is in destruction mode. He thinks he is winning the battle.

No one can live well with such a heart. A heart has to be restored to health to sustain life.

Ask advice from the Great Physician, Jesus. Listen to His Word. Hear His voice through His servants who minister to you. Reach out to Him. Restore communication with God, your Father.

Don't expect God to meet your list of expectations. Instead, endeavor to meet His desire for you. Of course, you will pray and ask for things, but if His answer is *no* or *wait*, don't give up. He does have the best plan in mind for you. He is your ultimate Mentor and does know more than you.

Do you remember when you first met God? Maybe you were a child. Most people don't truly know God until they have that first faith moment when only He could change things. Only God could have healed that person or situation, arranged such provision, or opened that door.

With God directing your life, everything was brighter. You even felt lighter because the burdens were lifted off you. You knew God was in control and would help you get through everything. Like many other relationships, that excitement can fade. Just as you can take a person for granted, you can take God for granted also. Instead of following His direction, you expect Him to follow you and bless your plans.

But I have this complaint against you. You don't love me or each other as you did at first! Look how far you have fallen! Turn back to me and do the works you did at first.   (Revelation 2:4–5 NLT)

To heal your heart, you have to collect all of those pieces of it that you gave away over the years to people who don't deserve that power over your well-being. I'm not talking about the love for your parents, your siblings, your friends, or anyone else near and dear to you. I'm talking about those acquaintances who walked out of your life with a piece of you. Collect those pieces of your heart.

YOUR HEART BELONGS TO GOD

Your heart—all of it—truly belongs only to God. He wants, needs, and deserves your entire heart. He causes it to function. It is His gift to everything you are. Once you realize this, you truly allow His life and love to flow through you to others.

Just as you expect intimacy with your spouse, expect intimacy with your Father. He knows you better than any other person on earth. He knows everything you have ever done, everything you have said, and everything you have thought, good *and* bad. *And He loves you unconditionally.*

God knows you are not perfect and He doesn't expect you to be. Just making the effort, taking the next step toward Him, is enough for God to reach out His hand. He loves you and forgives all of your mistakes. He doesn't dwell on those things you did that you have been holding on to for so long. He has forgiven you. Accept that and go on with Him.

Here's a prayer to collect your heart and give it totally to God:

Father, I have allowed pieces of my heart to scatter among so many people through the years. Forgive me, Father. I should have my whole heart available to only You. I claim all those broken and shattered pieces and order them to come back to their first love, Father—You! In Jesus's name, amen.

Guard Your Heart

Don't worry about anything; instead, pray about everything. Tell God what you need, and thank him for all he has done. Then you will experience God's peace, which exceeds anything we can understand. His peace will guard your hearts and minds as you live in Christ Jesus.

(Philippians 4:6–7 NLT)

Cast Your Cares to God

Give all your worries and cares to God, for he cares about you.

(1 Peter 5:7 NLT*)*

He Knows What You Need

Do not seek what you should eat or what you should drink, nor have an anxious mind. For all these things the nations of the world seek after, and your Father knows that you need these things. But seek the kingdom of God, and all these things shall be added to you. Do not fear, little flock, for it is your Father's good pleasure to give you the kingdom.

(Luke 12:29–32)

He Supplies Everything

Therefore I say to you, do not worry about your life, what you will eat or what you will drink; nor about your body, what you will put on. Is not life more than food and the body more than clothing? Look at the birds of the air, for they neither sow nor reap nor gather into barns; yet your heavenly Father feeds them. Are you not of more value than they?

(Matthew 6:25–26)

And Offers Abundant Life

The thief does not come except to steal, and to kill, and to destroy. I have come that they may have life, and that they may have it more abundantly. *(John 10:10)*

NO, LIFE ISN'T PERFECT

Some parts of life just hurt. There is no getting around it or avoiding it. Bumps and scrapes come with the journey. How you handle them is the key! Like any other part of life, you have a very important choice each day. How are you going to respond to your battle?

What if the first stumble made a toddler stop trying to walk? Or if a scraped knee after a fall while running or learning to ride a bicycle prevented a child from enjoying outdoor activities? Imagine how many fun life experiences would be missed.

Some feel challenged by a negative situation while others decide their goal is unreachable and give up. However, persevering and finding a way around or through challenges can result in new inventions and medical breakthroughs. Ben Franklin tested thousands of materials to create an incandescent light bulb. If he'd given up, imagine how many years it would take for another inventor of his caliber to come along. Why, it's possible that we'd have no cell phones or Internet!

WHAT'S YOUR IDEA?

Suppose you have an idea and investigate the possibility of creating something new. If it's been done before, can you make it better, easier, or cheaper? If it's an original concept, how can you make your idea work? It can be a piece of equipment, a machine, a clothing item, or a recipe—anything you can think of.

Books, encyclopedias, websites, and how-to books are everywhere as people freely share their ideas. Find a class on any subject you are interested in. Try out new hobbies. If you could do anything in the world, what would you do? You are free to go and do whatever you desire!

What is stopping you? God has given you an incredible mind. Your imagination is no accident. Made in the image of God who created all things, you have a creative mind and should be using it every day. How do you develop it or open it to the possibilities of life?

WELCOME OTHERS INTO YOUR LIFE

God created man for relationship. We need each other. Communication, attention, affirmation, love, touch, assistance, help—God needs us just as much as we need Him. Think about it. Who shares God's love on earth? Who spreads His Word around the world? Who created TV to cover the earth with His Word? Who chooses to worship Him and praise Him for His endless blessings?

Open the door. Break down the barriers surrounding you. Welcome other people into your space. Understand the Creator. Listen to your Father. Allow the Holy Spirit to work through you. Share Him with others. Give others a chance to follow you out into the world.

There are many self-help books on the market. Some may even classify this book in that genre, but what I share is much different. Yes, you have to pick it up, read it, and absorb what I say, but then you simply have to accept what is already available to you: God's love.

Through Him, you can break down the walls. Through His healing love, you can be whole again. With His Holy Spirit living within you, you can be everything He designed for you to be. He has special plans for you. You just have to accept them and enjoy living them out.

WE CAN ALL DO BETTER

Most people believe they are good and doing their best, but with God's assistance, *everyone* can do better. God created each precious person with their own talents and abilities, which have to be discovered and developed with wisdom and understanding. God has placed gifts within you. Allow Him to guide you toward your areas of strength.

> *"As* [a man] *thinks in his heart, so is he."*   (Proverbs 23:7)

Everyone seems to lose control of their temper at times. What comes out of their mouth shows what is buried in their heart. It might be what they're really thinking or feeling about *that* situation, or it might be the release of pent-up anger or frustration from another situation entirely.

If you are around a person 24/7, you will probably see more than you expected or ever wanted to know. Newlyweds are almost always in for some surprises. A spouse may not be the happy, cheerful optimist you thought they were. Everyone gets tired and perhaps irritated at times. A negative word or attitude may escape into the atmosphere. Tempers flare, hurtful words are spoken. Apologies are in order to calm the waters and restore peace.

SEEK THE FRUIT OF THE SPIRIT

No matter what, you should strive to treat everyone with kindness, gentleness, and peace. One of the challenges of the Christian life is to allow the seeds of the fruit of the Spirit take root within your heart and permit them to develop into the controlling force of your behavior. The following verses cite the bad fruit:

> *Now the works of the flesh are evident, which are: adultery, fornication, uncleanness, lewdness, idolatry, sorcery, hatred, contentions, jealousies, outbursts of wrath, selfish ambitions, dissensions, heresies, envy, murders, drunkenness, revelries, and the like; of which I tell you beforehand, just as I also told you in time past, that those who practice such things will not inherit the kingdom of God.*   (Galatians 5:19–21)

If you recognize these things in your life, or in someone else's, you have some work to do to be more like Jesus, the Holy Spirit, and the Father. Since we are made *"in the image of God"* (Genesis 1:27), these negative things should be avoided at all costs.

> But the fruit of the Spirit is love, joy, peace, longsuffering, kindness, goodness, faithfulness, gentleness, self-control. Against such there is no law.
>
> (Galatians 5:22–23)

The fruit of the Spirit shows all of the wonderful attributes of God, what we should be striving to emulate in our earthly lives.

Read these verses carefully. Which fruit are you feeling? Which ones do you show to others? Which ones need work, pruning, feeding, or watering?

What words come out of your mouth? Can you use gentler words to get your ideas understood? Can you control the tone of your voice or lower the volume? Is there a more productive and encouraging way to accomplish your goal?

If your words are angry and hurtful, think of the pain you are causing the other person. They may be building their wall to protect themselves from you. Remember how *you* felt when someone spoke cruel, ugly words to you, gave you a strange look, or shouted at you. It hurt, didn't it? Decide in your heart to never hurt another person the way you were hurt.

A TREE IS KNOWN BY ITS FRUIT

Are the words coming from your mouth good fruit...or bad fruit?

> Either make the tree good and its fruit good, or else make the tree bad and its fruit bad; for a tree is known by its fruit. Brood of vipers! How can you, being evil, speak good things? For out of the abundance of the heart the mouth speaks. A good man out of the good treasure of his heart brings forth good things, and an evil man out of the evil treasure brings forth evil things. But I say to you that for every idle word men may speak, they will give account of it in the day of judgment.   (Matthew 12:33–36)

These are very important keys to Christian living. Gentleness, kindness, patience...if you are not displaying these characteristics, reassess your commitment to God. If He is in control, bitterness, resentment, hate, and anger will not be used to describe you ever again.

Meekness does not mean weakness! It actually takes a lot of strength to hold your tongue when you want to yell back at a person or a situation in retaliation when something wrong or hurtful has been said or done. Your *old man* might still be inside you, itching for the opportunity to get out and yell. Count to ten, ask God for His control, and hold your tongue.

Consider what Jesus would do in every situation. Every Christian is called to act like Jesus, the One who lives within you.

Fear, pain, or unbelief may cause restless, sleepless nights, but once you accept God's love and walk in His peace, you will experience His restorative rest as He dispatches His angels to handle your problems while you sleep.

THE TRUTH WILL SET YOU FREE

Then Jesus said to those Jews who believed Him, "If you abide in My word, you are My disciples indeed. And you shall know the truth, and the truth shall make you free." (John 8:31–32)

Accept the truth you are learning and apply it to your life. The next time you don't know what to do, remember this verse. Find your Bible and start reading. God will answer you.

Truth won't prevent all problems or hardships of life. Life happens—the good and the bad. But it will have a remarkable effect on how you live through each day. You will become a living witness of His love to all who are watching your reaction to adversity. They will come to you for answers when they face their own battles.

Jesus said to him, "I am the way, the truth, and the life. No one comes to the Father except through Me. (John 14:6)

God is Truth and He always brings freedom and healing, especially of the heart.

If then you were raised with Christ, seek those things which are above, where Christ is, sitting at the right hand of God. Set your mind on things above, not on things on the earth. (Colossians 3:1–2)

Think on heavenly things, not earthly ones. What would God want you to do in every situation today?

STEP 6: REACH OUT

There is not one human on this earth who can say, "I am feeling fine!" all day, every day. Life isn't like that. Disappointments, disease, death, and pain are all around us. If troubles are not affecting you or your family today, a neighbor or a friend is dealing with them.

We are designed to help one another. Part of your rehabilitation for your own issues is to be aware of others, recognize what they are going through, and reach out in love and compassion to help them. If you have never suffered, you truly can't minister to a hurting soul.

What are the symptoms or outward characteristics of a hurting or damaged heart? If you want to minister to others, you will need to know what to look for. If you are in a recovery or rehabilitation stage of healing your own heart, you may recognize these symptoms almost unconsciously.

Fear is probably the most common. Someone with a broken heart may shrink back if another tries to touch them. If ministering to such a person, always ask permission to touch them. They may not look at you in the eye. Their head may be down with their eyes looking at the floor or just peeking up at you occasionally. They may speak in a whisper. They may panic and run until they get enough courage to return.

They will probably sit in the back and come to the altar last in line when most others are gone. They will sit alone near an easily accessible exit and watch everyone with a wary eye.

If you have ever been freed from fear, shame, or a broken heart, you will recognize the behavior. Minister gently. They probably haven't been able to trust anyone for a long time and desperately need the love and touch of God.

If you are ministering at a meeting, move the microphone away from them. They are usually ashamed and don't want anyone to know about their problem. You may need to sit with them away from the crowd; however, they may not want to go with you alone to another room. Ask if they would be more comfortable moving away from the center of attention in front of everyone. Go to chairs on the side of the room for privacy.

LISTEN TO GOD'S VOICE

Accept God's Word, accept His Son and the Holy Spirit living within you. Listen to His sweet voice. Obey His Word. Peace like a river will truly flood over your soul and wash over those around you.

The enemy will still try to sit on your shoulder and whisper, "Oh, what about the time you did that…" or "You weren't really healed. That was just emotion!" Just laugh at the enemy! Tell him, "Talk to my big brother, Jesus!"

Keep your boundaries up and spiritual armor intact. Remember, *you* have an assignment from God. Stay physically and spiritually healthy so you can fight the battle and enjoy the victory.

Love is the basis of all healing—and God is love. (See 1 John 4.) Love cures loneliness, erases pain, and obliterates hate.

Listen, love, and learn. Each individual who comes to you will have a story to tell, hurts to release, and pain to heal. Once their hidden scars are healed in the name of Jesus, their countenance will change, their physical appearance will change, their eyes will sparkle, and joy will bubble out of them.

DEALING WITH CELLULAR MEMORY

Trauma affects a lot of people and the only way you can get rid of it is through prayer. There is no way a doctor is going to go in and scrape trauma and stress off of your cells. Only God can heal you. The trauma can even exist on a cellular level. Let me give you a few examples of what I'm talking about.

There's a story about a lady who had a heart problem and needed a transplant. She was so happy after she got the call and received a donor's heart. During her first night of sleep, however, she had a horrific nightmare that she was being stabbed to death. The same dream returned night after night. She spoke to the police and a sketch artist drew a composite of the killer in her nightmare. It turned out to be her heart donor's murderer. He was found, convicted, and sent to prison. The trauma happened to another, but it affected this woman, too.

Many times following a transplant, a patient has knowledge of the donor's experiences before death. These are all documented medically.

Here's another story: I met a heart transplant patient who kept having nightmares about a Texas license plate. Night after night, a vision of it woke her up. Finally, the police were called and they traced the license plate to the vehicle's owner—the heart donor's uncle. He agreed to let police examine the car and they found blood stains in the trunk matching the heart donor's DNA. Apparently, the uncle had thrown her body into the trunk and as she was dying, she kept thinking about the license plate. That man is in jail today.

One of the partners of the 4 Corners Alliance had a friend who needed a kidney transplant and got the call that one was available. On the way to the hospital, they wondered where this kidney had come from. There had been a horrendous murder the night before, so the partner wanted to pray about the transplant. She laid hands on the container holding the kidney and said, "I command that all traumas leave this kidney before it goes into my friend's body."

The surgery was perfect. That donated kidney just went in with minimal swelling, almost like God did it. There was no trauma, nightmares, or infection.

Death, major surgery, combat, abuse—all can cause trauma and stress. I curse it in Jesus's name and any effect that it has had on the body. I speak it to be completely turned around and the body to be restored, in Jesus's name. When you pray for someone in the name of Jesus, curse the spirit of trauma and command that it be gone. Continue by ordering their body's chemicals and electrical and magnetic frequencies to go back into normal alignment.

HEALING THE WHOLE MAN

In my book, *Healing the Whole Man Handbook*, I have a chapter on the body's electrical and magnetic frequencies.[7] Understanding this concept is important because when these frequencies are out of balance, the immune system is compromised. I pray for my immune system every day, saying, "In the name of Jesus, I thank You that my immune system is doing what it is supposed to be doing."

Abnormal electrical and magnetic frequencies can cause a physical earthquake within your own body. We do not have the original frequencies that pull on our bodies as did Adam and Eve. Some people wear magnetic necklaces, bracelets, shoes, soles, and other items to get their body back into proper electrical and magnetic balance.

You may not be able to take those when you travel, but you can take prayer anywhere. Just pray, "In the name of Jesus, I command my body to be in perfect harmony and balance electrically and magnetically." See how simple that is? It's a whole lot less expensive, too. Each of us needs to do what we can do to keep our bodies in proper balance.

---

7. Joan Hunter, *Healing the Whole Man Handbook: Effective Prayers for Body, Soul, and Spirit* (New Kensington, PA: Whitaker House, 2005).

COMMAND TRAUMA TO LEAVE

Several years ago, I lost both my parents. After my mother died, I was told Dad would be gone in three to six days. Grief and trauma overwhelmed me on the eve of the fifth day. I basically lost my voice, which is one of the first signs of trauma attacking your body. When I got to my hotel room, I took a shower while I cried out to God as loud as I could, which wasn't much with no voice.

As I was saying, "In the name of Jesus," I realized what was happening to me. Trauma and grief were trespassing. They could not stay in my body—I had a television show scheduled in the morning and my voice needed to be normal. I said, "In the name of Jesus, I curse the spirit of trauma. I curse the spirit of grief and I command it to be gone. I command my voice to be completely restored in Jesus's name."

As I finished by declaring, "Hallelujah," my voice was 100 percent back to normal. My vocal cords, my trouble with the grief, the heaviness—all that junk was lifted off me. Don't misunderstand: I missed my parents and still do. But the heaviness and the grief were gone.

If I had not dealt with that very quickly, I would not be here today because that grief and trauma could have crippled me. Since that day, I can share from my personal experience.

After you read this book, more than likely, somewhere in your life, you will experience trauma. It's up to you to recognize the symptoms and take the steps you are learning to stay trauma free.

TROUBLES WILL COME...

Jesus said, *"Here on earth you will have many trials and sorrows. But take heart, because I have overcome the world"* (John 16:33 NLT). Praying for trauma and grief to leave doesn't mean you have to forget about the cause, nor does it mean you will never be hurt again.

I miss telling my mom about the incredible miracles that happen in my life. I miss telling her, "I went to Haiti, Mom, and it was the biggest crusade that had ever happened in my ministry." I miss telling her what God is doing during my meetings. Everywhere I go, people tell me about healings or baptism of the Holy Ghost they received in one of my parents' services. Mom and Dad always grinned when they heard about these testimonies.

I miss that neither of them were at my daughters' weddings or here to welcome their great-grandchildren into this world. Every once in a while, I'll cry about things like that, but I don't have the heaviness, the grief, or the trauma. There is a difference.

Know beyond a shadow of a doubt that you can remain trauma-free. Sad situations will happen. People you love are going to die and the longer you live, the more likely that will be. You will die and so will I, but praise God, I'm going to meet my Savior and my parents in heaven.

ACID-ALKALINE BALANCE

When a body is under stress, it produces excess acid, which causes an abnormal pH balance. The pH stands for "power of hydrogen," a measurement of the body's hydrogen concentration, and pH balance refers to the alkalinity/acidity in our blood. If you don't have the proper amount of alkaline in your body, you can experience acid reflux. Too much acid in your body can also cause numerous health issues. You need to command the acid level to go down and the pH level to return to a proper balance in the neutral range.

We recently did an interesting test at a seminar I was teaching. First, we measured the pH level in our saliva, then we ingested a small amount of lemon juice. Five minutes later, we checked our pH level again. The lemon juice should have caused the pH strip to register a higher acidity level. However, some people, including me, had a neutral pH reading, showing how well we handle stress and the strength of our bodies' immune systems.

One lady even gave a testimony, saying, "Mine came back perfect because I read Joan Hunter's book *Power to Heal.*"[8]

I have been through many opportunities to overcome stress. I know what to do when it comes and how to get rid of it. By the way, getting rid of stress does *not* mean getting rid of your spouse.

TRAUMA'S EFFECTS DELAYED

Usually within six months to a year following a traumatic event, ill effects show up in your body. I wanted to go to Haiti after the earthquake before the sixth-month period was up. Praise God, I was there within the first four months. I prayed with them and trained seven hundred pastors. We went to orphanages, hospitals, and nurseries where the babies were being delivered in one big room.

---

8. Joan Hunter, *Power to Heal: Receiving God's Everyday Miracles* (New Kensington, PA: Whitaker House, 2009).

My ministry team and I prayed over these babies whose mothers were pregnant with them when the earthquake hit. We prayed that all the effects of the trauma be gone and they would be normal in Jesus's name.

Many adoptions were approved before the earthquake hit and right afterward, many babies were sent to homes in America. About six or seven months after these babies were adopted, they were exhibiting strange behaviors, screaming, biting, and hitting their adoptive parents. These poor children were suffering from trauma.

PRAYING FOR HEALING

Left in a Straitjacket

A few years ago when I was in Canada, a lady came up to me and asked for prayer. She said, "When I was a child, my parents couldn't keep me so they put me into an orphanage and then foster care."

When she was two or three, the orphanage put her in a bed because they had run out of cribs. She kept getting up at night because she wanted to see the other children—a very normal response. After a few nights of this, the caretakers decided to put her in a straitjacket to keep her in bed and then they strapped her in. She couldn't get up to go the bathroom until morning. This little girl was extremely traumatized.

I told the woman to cross her arms and hug her waist. She started screaming at me, "I can't! I can't!"

Very gently, I said, "If you'll give me about three minutes, you will be completely free." She then agreed to try and finally hugged herself. I told her I was going to squeeze her half to death, but she would be free. I placed my arms and hands where the straps of the straitjacket would have been and held her tightly while I prayed, "In the name of Jesus, I curse this spirit of trauma and I command it to go in Jesus's name." I released my hands and she crumpled to the floor.

Then she got up and with total amazement declared, "It's gone!" Her husband reached out to embrace her, but she started breathing heavily. He gently said, "That's okay. Don't worry about it. You are okay." For years and years, she hadn't been able to embrace him. After prayer, she was finally able to hug her husband. It was awesome. In grateful praise, she could also open her arms to Jesus. Hallelujah!

Carried Away by Street Cleaner

When we were in Northern Ireland, a lady requested prayer for her feet. She said, "My feet hurt so bad, I feel like I am walking on glass." She didn't have a wheelchair and was not capable of walking normally. Every step was painful. She had to wear shoes that were too big because her ankles were so swollen.

Many people had prayed for her without success, but no one had prayed against trauma. I asked when the pain started and she told me that several years prior, she was sitting in her car when a street cleaner came by, picked up her car, and started carrying it down the street. She panicked. She couldn't get out through the doors so she got on her back and kicked out the windshield. Of course, it shattered everywhere, but she was able to climb out. The trauma of that event remained imbedded in the cells of her feet.

I prayed, "In the name of Jesus, I curse this trauma and command it to be gone." Within seconds, she exclaimed, "Thank You, Jesus! Thank You, Jesus!" She repeatedly stomped her feet, amazed that the pain was gone. When she left, she couldn't keep her shoes on because her feet and ankles were no longer swollen.

Gauze Left Inside Throat

Another lady came up for prayer in Myrtle Beach. She explained, "I feel like I have something back in my throat and it's hard to swallow. I choke when I try to drink." Some time ago, this woman had surgery for a tongue reduction and when she was coming out of anesthesia, she told the nurse, "I can't breathe! I can't breathe!"

She was told that feeling is normal "because you had a tube down your throat."

She said, "I feel like I am strangling."

They said, "It is just the tube. Don't worry about it. It is a normal reaction."

She whispered, "I can't breathe." Just to pacify her, they looked inside… and found a piece of gauze had been left in her throat. With her tongue bleeding so much, the doctors had placed gauze there to catch the blood. They removed it, but her throat had already been traumatized.

I prayed, "In the name of Jesus, I command all that trauma to go in Jesus's name!" Someone handed her a glass of water and she said it was the best water she had tasted in years.

Childhood Trauma

Another story involves a guy I will call Frank. He came to a healing school to just watch. I prayed over him on Saturday afternoon and anointed him in Jesus's name. On Sunday morning, I found out that he was the church "psychophrenic." That's not a nice title, is it? Frank lived in a home where he had to be checked out and taken back within a certain time.

I was told on Sunday that he had schizophrenia. I said healing for that is easy for God because schizophrenia is brought on by trauma. It's a shield you can hide behind so people will leave you alone and not hurt you.

I prayed over Frank and my team member ministered to him. I said, "Father, in the name of Jesus, I curse this trauma. I command it to go and I curse the spirit of schizophrenia, in Jesus's name. I command the chemicals in this body to return to normal in Jesus's name. Thank You, Jesus. Amen."

After the service, the pastors were discussing Frank's situation with me. They explained that when he was three years old, his mother doused herself with gasoline, lit herself on fire, and burned to death while he watched. Then, his father got custody...and Frank's experience with Dad made what happened with his mother seem like nothing. He had a horrendous upbringing.

To escape those events, any of us might choose some kind of shell to hide in. Whether you call it psychophrenic or anything else, it's understandable why Frank would want to be left alone. He had been doing better because the church had been counseling him for over five years.

Frank came back for the Sunday night service. Monday was toenail-cutting day at his group home. Frank was allowed to help others who could not clip their own toenails. One guy was lying on the table and Frank noticed one leg was shorter than the other. It turned out this man had a back problem. Frank prayed for him and he was healed.

Frank was so excited, he could hardly stand it. He started hunting for someone else he could pray for. A lady came limping down the hall with a swollen ankle that had turned purple. She let Frank pray for her and the swelling disappeared and the ankle's color went back to normal.

Frank was completely set free from schizophrenia. Hallelujah! He said, "I know she prayed for me. I know she laid hands on me for healing. I really, really didn't think God would use me!"

But He did! And He can use you, too.

Afraid to Leave Home

One lady came to a Friday night meeting in Florida. She was diagnosed with agoraphobia, an anxiety disorder that can make you feel trapped. She was too afraid to come into the church, so she sat in the foyer with her service dog.

Fear kept her homebound most of the time because she believed that every time she went out, something terrible would happen. She only felt safe at home. She had a multimillion-dollar company that she ran from home with her computer and telephone. She lived a very lonely life. She needed to take her service dog even to go to her mailbox. She couldn't do anything by herself and couldn't handle crowds either.

I prayed for this woman in the lobby. I cursed the spirit of trauma and fear and commanded the agoraphobia to go in Jesus's name. She came back to the Sunday morning service by herself. Hallelujah! After church, she went to the grocery store. We go to the grocery store all the time and don't think anything of this. Just the fact that this woman could go to church and then to the store among a crowd of people was just awesome.

Fear of Abandonment

I was ministering at a church and a lady came for healing. Her husband was in the second or third row. I tried to talk to her and make eye contact, but she would only look at her husband. She had been married about forty-five years and was free of unforgiveness, but because of trauma and abandonment buried in her past, she was terrified that her husband was going to leave her while she was talking to me! During all those years of their marriage, every day that he went to work, she would experience a panic attack. When they went out and she needed to go to the restroom, he had to stand outside the door and talk to her to reassure her that he wasn't going to leave her there.

Talk about a controlling spirit of fear brought on by abandonment. That husband truly loved her to put up with this behavior for so many years. I prayed for her. A few days later, I got an email from her. Her husband wanted a newspaper so she got in her car and drove to the drugstore all by herself. The store wasn't open yet so she waited outside. Other cars pulled up. While she was waiting for the store to open, she knocked on a car window and said, "May I pray for you while we are waiting?" She prayed for all those people.

When the store opened, she went in, got the newspaper, and drove home saying, "I'm really healed!" If anything is needed, she can now leave her husband at home, get in the car, and go. She knows he will be there when she returns. A few months later, she drove a few hours to my meetings, every night, by herself. That's freedom.

Terrible Car Accidents

Very recently, we prayed for a lady whose car had been T-boned. Every part of her body was slammed into the car. There was nothing physically wrong with her even though her body was in excruciating pain. I did not pray for her healing. I said, "In the name of Jesus, I command every bit of the trauma that the left side of this body experienced to go in Jesus's name." The trauma left her and she went home smiling.

In another instance, a twenty-three-year-old lady came in for ministry. At age fourteen, she was in a car accident. Her head hit the dashboard, then hit the windshield, and her face was destroyed. Her body was so mangled that she hurt everywhere. Doctors said she would not be able to walk and would be a vegetable, but everyone in her church prayed for her.

Thanks to God and good surgeons, she's a gorgeous, tall, blonde lady without a scar on her face. You would never know she had been in a terrible accident. However, she remained in pain and the crash had caused her upper body to be shaped like a "C." We prayed for the trauma to go and for her body to go back into alignment. Her whole body was twisting and turning all over the place, but it ended up perfect.

Then she said, "Only one thing. I feel like I have something right here on my face like a mask." I put my hand on her face and I said, "Father, in the name of Jesus, I command that spirit of trauma to leave her face and I command that mask to be taken off in Jesus's name." And it was gone. She was totally set free because the spirit of trauma was gone! Amen!

THE POWER OF PRAYING FOR TRAUMA

Those are some examples of the effects of trauma on a body. One of the leaders of a church in Illinois said he had not slept in his bed for more than four years. Instead, he had to sleep in a chair. I said, "You haven't been prayed for the spirit of trauma." In the name of Jesus, I commanded the spirit of trauma to go. His trauma left, his pain left, and he has been sleeping in his bed ever since.

That's how simple and yet how strong praying for trauma is. In the past when I prayed for people to get healed, I had phenomenal results. But when

I learned about praying for the spirit of trauma, the number of people who were healed just jumped. I had been praying this way for many years, but I am bringing it more to the forefront because I am seeing the disabling effects of trauma so often. People are getting healed of this silent, but deadly condition.

My book *Power to Heal* devotes a whole chapter to getting rid of trauma and how to pray over trauma for yourself and every area of your life. Getting rid of trauma is really easier than you can imagine. Cling to our hope: Jesus. Understand that Jesus is our only hope. He will make everything easier. If you have experienced anything traumatic, then understanding this will help you.

A TRAUMATIC ATTACK

Until Kelley, my husband, started traveling with the ministry full-time, he had a full-time job where he worked from home. He had four boys who are all older now. One day, I called home and a man answered the phone. "Hello?"

I thought, *Oh God, not again, not again!* You could tell the effect it had on me. *Oh God, I don't want to go through this again! Oh God, help me! I just can't do this again.* I was speechless and that is very unusual for me. I was covered with fear and drama and my emotions exploded.

In a matter of moments, the person who answered the phone said, "Do you want me to get my dad for you?"

It was Kelley's son Curt; his voice had changed and I didn't know he was staying at the house with his dad. It was so traumatizing to me. The whole car filled up with trauma. I turned to those in the car with me and said, "You better pray, you better pray, you know I'm a wreck. He can't really understand why I am not in the mood to talk with him. And I am completely traumatized over nothing. How do you explain to a man that you are traumatized over nothing?"

Curt asked, "Why are you crying?"

I squeaked out, "I don't know; because I feel like it." It was a long time before I explained to him what had happened. It was embarrassing. I had discovered my ex-husband's secret life and lifestyle when a man called the house and I answered. Kelley would never do such a thing because it's totally not within his being. But a man answering our home phone while I was on the road was a trigger to past trauma in my life. Even though that voice belonged to my son, it was still a shock because I hadn't talked to him since his voice deepened.

The ladies traveling with me said, "You better pray for yourself. Now! Get your hand on your heart. Get rid of that trauma!"

And I did pray: "I rebuke the spirit of trauma and I command that it be gone in Jesus's name!"

Don't allow situations to fester. Having that kind of reaction shocked me, but you have to understand where I was coming from.

THE GATOR AND THE LITTLE GIRL

I'll give you another story. I was born and raised in the Miami area. We lived near a herpetarium—a place for reptiles. I was friends with the owner's daughter Nina. We were playing at her house one day when an eight-foot alligator got loose and started coming through the house. When they want to, gators can run more than 30 miles an hour for a short distance. Little five-year-old girls are not going to outrun an alligator. I was scared half out of my wits. We quickly went into a room, got behind the door, and shut it. We were safe but still scared.

A few years ago, I went to a book conference in Orlando, Florida. Suddenly, the loudspeaker announced, "I just want you to know that there is an alligator running around the floor."

While I am trying to say, "Hi, Mr. So-and-So, I'm really glad to meet you," I'm envisioning this ten-foot, two-thousand-pound creature chasing me. I felt panic creeping in. The two people with me started hunting for this thing, but we couldn't find it.

Finally, we heard that the alligator was at a booth on the other side of the building. I was determined to see the animal that set off the trigger of panic within me.

Well, the alligator was a promotional stunt. It certainly attracted me to that booth! It was only four feet long and its mouth was securely taped shut. The vendor smiled as she said, "You can hold it if you want to."

I now know, from firsthand experience, that an alligator's belly is unbelievably soft and that's why alligator shoes are so soft. I actually held that alligator. At first, my face showed my fear, but then I relaxed. I had the experience of a lifetime.

GET RID OF TRAUMA NOW

Okay, put your hands on your heart. It's time we got rid of all the trauma in your life no matter what caused it. Whether you were molested as a child, verbally abused by a parent or teacher, experienced divorce or a loved one's death, or were in a war zone and watched a friend die or lost a limb, you can command that trauma to leave.

I had to pray more than once against trauma when my ex-husband left me for another man. I had to get rid of the repressed trauma when I was chased by an alligator. You may be unaware of some instances of trauma until a trigger pops up and you get the opportunity to deal with it again. This time, you know what to do and what to say!

This one simple prayer will cover it all, but I encourage you, after today, to pray over yourself again and be more specific. Father, in the name of Jesus, I send the word of healing to each one who is reading this today.

> Father, right now, in the name of Jesus, I curse this spirit of trauma to be gone. I command it to be gone in Jesus's name. I curse any feelings of abandonment, rejection, abuse, or worthlessness; I command every bit of that to go. I curse any spirits of hopelessness, depression, and oppression, and I command that to be gone in Jesus's name. I speak life, health, wholeness, and complete restoration in this life in Jesus's name. Amen.

You will now discover that some of the diseases that you had are gone. Trauma caused a lot of those conditions. With the trauma gone, the disease is gone. Now you are no longer feeding the trauma. Allow happy hormones, the endorphins, to rebuild your immune system.

Stress and trauma will affect your physical height, too. Many times, I have prayed for people to be healed of trauma and stress affecting their neck and shoulders. Suddenly, they are an inch or two taller because the stress had affected their stature. When the trauma and the effect of the stress leave, the body returns to its proper height.

HELP IS AVAILABLE FOR STRESS

Stress is part of life. What matters the most is how you handle it. The best thing you can do to prevent stress overload and the health consequences that come with it is to know your stress symptoms and get help as soon as possible.

Maybe you need to incorporate physical exercise to relieve your stress. Some find an outlet writing books that help others cope with their issues. Serving others in general can counter stress. Consider organizing activities for children in need, helping the lonely or disabled with housework or yardwork, offering transportation to get groceries or medical attention, visiting the injured who remain in the hospital, or volunteering at a food bank. Many churches have specially designed groups to help others, so whether you need help or want to help others, a church is always a good place to start.

If you are feeling overwhelmed by stress, talk to your doctor. Many symptoms of stress can be signs of other health problems. Your doctor can evaluate your symptoms and rule out other conditions. If stress is to blame, your doctor can recommend a therapist or counselor.

My first suggestion is always prayer and my office prayer partners are available during office hours Monday through Friday. We don't do phone counseling so if you need added assistance, find a Christian counselor for ongoing help. Often, our office can recommend someone in your area for personal ministry. Going to God should be the first step on your list.

GIVE YOUR WORRIES TO GOD

Several years ago, I used a very practical example of stress or worry relief. As I gave this instruction, one of my staff started to pile heavy books in my arms. These books represented my worries, concerns, and stress in general. Pretty soon, I had to sit down with my arms propped on a table. Then the books were piled in my lap. I physically could not manage all the extra weight being placed on me. I had to do something or collapse under the stress. The answer to my instruction that day was to give it all to God.

God once told me, "If you are ministering to My children as I direct you to, I will minister to and take care of your family, employees, business, and prayer requests." Since then, I just give Him all my concerns. I know He can take much better care of them, my needs, and prayer requests than I could.

Now, it's your turn. If you are concerned and burdened with stress, give each issue to Him. *"Give all your worries and cares to God, for he cares about you"* (1 Peter 5:7 NLT). He is always thinking about you and watching everything that concerns you. Lay all your cares and issues at the foot of the cross. Don't sneak back and pick them up again. Leave them all with Father God. He is in control. Nothing ever alters or changes until you lay it on the altar.

Stress hormones cause problems with your immune system, which affects your body's ability to fight illness. Then you get sick, become depressed, and feel hopeless, which brings more health issues. I once heard someone say,

"One minute of anger weakens the immune system for four or five hours. One minute of laughter boosts the immune system for twenty-four hours."

When you deal with trauma, you have to nip it in the bud, curse the trauma, curse the stress, and curse anything that may have brought that on like grief, loss, rejection, or abuse. Because you don't want any mental or spiritual trauma coming in to attack your body, you curse the spirit of trauma, curse the bipolar, command the chemicals to return to harmony and balance, and curse any addiction to medicinal drugs. Watch how quickly you can get off those drugs. Many do not need them anymore because they are healed.

Before my husband started traveling with me, if I had to worry about what he was doing, I would essentially be carrying him on my shoulders. He is too big of a guy for me to be doing that. I can't carry the weight of my husband, four children, four bonus sons, grandchildren, sons-in-law, all my staff—just thinking about it is exhausting. Not to mention writing books, the ministry, our home, and prayer partners around the world. I do sleep, not enough, but I do sleep. I choose not to worry about anything because it's all on the altar. Start laying all your concerns there and see how light your load will become.

SOME SUGGESTIONS

- Get connected with a Bible-based church
- Join a support group; many churches offer them
- Keep in touch regularly with family and friends
- Relocate to a safer neighborhood if necessary
- Maintain a regular exercise program
- Get involved with community services and help others in need
- Seek out mental health counseling if necessary

SPECIFIC TREATMENTS

The medical profession advocates medications and psychotherapy for anyone suffering from PTSD. Some get relief with medications and some do best talking about issues in group therapy. Anyone with PTSD has to find what works for them. As far as I'm concerned, Jesus offers the best cure.

If your environment is not safe, you need to move to a better one. If your loved one is threatening to hurt someone or themselves, they may need intervention to maintain safety for themselves and others around them.

Keeping a journal is often a good way to release stress and record progress back to normalcy. Surround yourself with favorite movies and books. Have a list of people to contact when your emotions seem to be overwhelming.

Avoid situations that you know can trigger high-powered emotions of anger or frustration. Walk away before things get out of control. Nothing positive gets accomplished in the heat of anger.

> *Choose for yourselves this day whom you will serve.... But as for me and my house, we will serve the* LORD. (Joshua 24:15)

ASK YOURSELF...

Here are some questions to ask yourself during each day:

+ Can I glorify Christ by listening to this song? Watching this program? Looking at this website?

+ Are the people around me helping me or dragging me downward?

+ What is the best and most productive thing I can do today?

+ Am I keeping my mind fixed on the Lord or am I getting distracted by the enemy?

GARBAGE IN, GARBAGE OUT

What you allow into your life, your mind, or your body must eventually come out. Concentrate on positive things and reject the negative. That includes people, TV, radio, books, and everything else.

Some people can't talk for more than five minutes and I can tell what they have been doing, watching, hearing, or reading. If you take in the garbage of the world, sooner or later, it will manifest in your life in a negative manner. Keep your mind focused on the goodness of God and that is what people will see and hear when you open your mouth.

Choose. Choose life. Choose His life.

★ 17 ★
POSITIONED-TO-WIN
SCRIPTURES

Victory with healing, recovery, and life in general comes with a commitment to and faith in God. When you need encouragement, go to His Word. It is available 24/7 when your mentor, friend, or spouse is not. Read these Scripture passages. It is best to read them out loud so you hear the words as well as see them. This is not an extensive listing of God's beautiful promises. You can certainly do your own research and add to this list to fit your situation.

When the Bible mentions the *enemy*, remember it is talking about Satan and his minions—the spirits of depression, death, pain, destruction, fear, anger, and everything else trying to hurt you. Satan's job is to destroy you. God's job is to save you. You choose!

After reading each Scripture passage, pause for a minute. How does it relate to your particular situation? Jot down your thoughts in the space following the Scripture verses. Maybe you want to only work on one or two Scriptures a day. Again, it is your choice.

KEEP FIGHTING TO TOTAL VICTORY
God is showing me just how essential it is that we have determination as we serve Him. Too many Christians quit and give up way too easily. I encourage you to fight the good fight of faith and press on to victory.

One thing I do, forgetting those things which are behind and reaching forward to those things which are ahead, I press toward the goal for the prize of the upward call of God in Christ Jesus.   (Philippians 3:13–14)

For I know the plans I have for you, declares the LORD, plans for welfare and not for evil, to give you a future and a hope.   (Jeremiah 29:11 ESV)

_____

_____

_____

SALVATION

If we confess our sins, He is faithful and just to forgive us our sins and to cleanse us from all unrighteousness. (1 John 1:9)

Jesus answered him, "Truly, truly, I say to you, unless one is born again he cannot see the kingdom of God." (John 3:3 ESV)

Then Peter said to them, "Repent, and let every one of you be baptized in the name of Jesus Christ for the remission of sins; and you shall receive the gift of the Holy Spirit. For the promise is to you and to your children, and to all who are afar off, as many as the Lord our God will call." (Acts 2:38–39)

And we know that God causes everything to work together for the good of those who love God and are called according to his purpose for them. (Romans 8:28 NLT)

I have told you all this so that you may have peace in me. Here on earth you will have many trials and sorrows. But take heart, because I have overcome the world. (John 16:33 NLT)

For whatever is born of God overcomes the world. And this is the victory that has overcome the world—our faith. Who is he who overcomes the world, but he who believes that Jesus is the Son of God? (1 John 5:4–5)

Thanks be to God, who gives us the victory through our Lord Jesus Christ. (1 Corinthians 15:57)

Now I know that the LORD saves His anointed; He will answer him from His holy heaven with the saving strength of His right hand. (Psalm 20:6)

The LORD is my light and my salvation; whom shall I fear? The LORD is the strength of my life; of whom shall I be afraid? (Psalm 27:1)

The LORD will keep you from all evil; he will keep your life. The LORD will keep your going out and your coming in from this time forth and forevermore. (Psalm 121:7–8 ESV)

Do not rejoice over me, my enemy; when I fall, I will arise; when I sit in darkness, the LORD will be a light to me. (Micah 7:8)

Who shall separate us from the love of Christ? Shall tribulation, or distress, or persecution, or famine, or nakedness, or peril, or sword?... In all these things we are more than conquerors through Him who loved us.

(Romans 8:35, 37)

It is impossible to please God without faith. Anyone who wants to come to him must believe that God exists and that he rewards those who sincerely seek him. (Hebrews 11:6 NLT)

Don't be afraid, for I am with you. Don't be discouraged, for I am your God. I will strengthen you and help you. I will hold you up with my victorious right hand. (Isaiah 41:10 NLT)

So we do not lose heart. Though our outer self is wasting away, our inner self is being renewed day by day. For this light momentary affliction is preparing for us an eternal weight of glory beyond all comparison, as we look not to the things that are seen but to the things that are unseen. For the things that are seen are transient, but the things that are unseen are eternal. (2 Corinthians 4:16–18 ESV)

I have been crucified with Christ; it is no longer I who live, but Christ lives in me; and the life which I now live in the flesh I live by faith in the Son of God, who loved me and gave Himself for me. (Galatians 2:20)

The LORD says, "I will rescue those who love me. I will protect those who trust in my name. When they call on me, I will answer; I will be with them in trouble. I will rescue and honor them. I will reward them with a long life and give them my salvation." (Psalm 91:14–16 NLT)

Those who trust in the LORD are like Mount Zion, which cannot be moved, but abides forever. As the mountains surround Jerusalem, so the LORD surrounds His people from this time forth and forever.

(Psalm 125:1–2)

Rejoice because your names are written in heaven. (Luke 10:20)

_____

_____

_____

AVOID USING SPEECH AS A WEAPON

Rejoice in the Lord always. Again I will say, rejoice!... Finally, brethren, whatever things are true, whatever things are noble, whatever things are just, whatever things are pure, whatever things are lovely, whatever things are of good report, if there is any virtue and if there is anything praiseworthy—meditate on these things. (Philippians 4:4, 8)

Pleasant words are like a honeycomb, sweetness to the soul and health to the bones. (Proverbs 16:24)

Let no corrupting talk come out of your mouths, but only such as is good for building up, as fits the occasion, that it may give grace to those who hear. (Ephesians 4:29 ESV)

Let your conversation be gracious and attractive so that you will have the right response for everyone. (Colossians 4:6 NLT)

_____

_____

_____

RESIST TEMPTATION

Ralph Waldo Emerson wrote, "Man becomes what he thinks about all day long."

No temptation has overtaken you that is not common to man. God is faithful, and he will not let you be tempted beyond your ability, but with the temptation he will also provide the way of escape, that you may be able to endure it. (1 Corinthians 10:13 ESV)

Blessed is the man who endures temptation; for when he has been approved, he will receive the crown of life which the Lord has promised to those who love Him. (James 1:12)

For I consider that the sufferings of this present time are not worthy to be compared with the glory which shall be revealed in us. (Romans 8:18)

For we do not have a High Priest who cannot sympathize with our weaknesses, but was in all points tempted as we are, yet without sin. (Hebrews 4:15)

Stay alert! Watch out for your great enemy, the devil. He prowls around like a roaring lion, looking for someone to devour. Stand firm against him, and be strong in your faith. Remember that your family of believers all over the world is going through the same kind of suffering you are.

(1 Peter 5:8–9 NLT)

VICTORY

For whatever is born of God overcomes the world. And this is the victory that has overcome the world—our faith. (1 John 5:4)

David said to the Philistine, "You come to me with a sword, with a spear, and with a javelin. But I come to you in the name of the LORD of hosts, the God of the armies of Israel, whom you have defied. This day the LORD will deliver you into my hand, and I will strike you and take your head from you. And this day I will give the carcasses of the camp of the Philistines to the birds of the air and the wild beasts of the earth, that all the earth may know that there is a God in Israel. Then all this assembly shall know that the LORD does not save with sword and spear; for the battle is the LORD's, and He will give you into our hands." (1 Samuel 17:45–47)

The horse is prepared for the day of battle, but the victory belongs to the LORD. (Proverbs 21:31 NLT)

The LORD your God is going with you! He will fight for you against your enemies, and he will give you victory! (Deuteronomy 20:4 NLT)

GIFTS OF THE SPIRIT

There are different kinds of spiritual gifts, but the same Spirit is the source of them all.... A spiritual gift is given to each of us so we can help each other. To one person the Spirit gives the ability to give wise advice; to another the same Spirit gives a message of special knowledge. The same Spirit gives great faith to another, and to someone else the one Spirit gives the gift of healing. He gives one person the power to perform miracles, and another the ability to prophesy. He gives someone else the ability to discern whether a message is from the Spirit of God or from another spirit. Still another person is given the ability to speak in unknown languages, while another is given the ability to interpret what is being said. It is the one and only Spirit who distributes all these gifts. He alone decides which gift each person should have. (1 Corinthians 12:4, 7–11 NLT)

_____

_____

_____

LIVING HOLY LIVES

Since we have these promises, beloved, let us cleanse ourselves from every defilement of body and spirit, bringing holiness to completion in the fear of God. (2 Corinthians 7:1 ESV)

Do not be conformed to this world, but be transformed by the renewing of your mind, that you may prove what is that good and acceptable and perfect will of God. (Romans 12:2)

You shall be holy, for I the LORD your God am holy. (Leviticus 19:2)

That the God of our Lord Jesus Christ, the Father of glory, may give to you the spirit of wisdom and revelation in the knowledge of Him, the eyes of your understanding being enlightened; that you may know what is the hope of His calling, what are the riches of the glory of His inheritance in the saints, and what is the exceeding greatness of His power toward us who believe, according to the working of His mighty power. (Ephesians 1:17–19)

_____

_____

_____

GOD'S DIRECTION

Trust in the Lord with all your heart; do not depend on your own understanding. Seek his will in all you do, and he will show you which path to take. (Proverbs 3:5–6 NLT)

_____

_____

TRUST GOD

Trust in the Lord, and do good; dwell in the land, and feed on His faithfulness. Delight yourself also in the Lord, and He shall give you the desires of your heart. Commit your way to the Lord, trust also in Him, and He shall bring it to pass. He shall bring forth your righteousness as the light, and your justice as the noonday. (Psalm 37:3–6)

Jesus Christ is the same yesterday, today, and forever. (Hebrews 13:8)

O Lord of hosts, blessed is the one who trusts in you! (Psalm 84:12 ESV)

I pray that God, the source of hope, will fill you completely with joy and peace because you trust in him. Then you will overflow with confident hope through the power of the Holy Spirit. (Romans 15:13 NLT)

_____

_____

GOD'S PROMISES

Come to Me, all you who labor and are heavy laden, and I will give you rest. Take My yoke upon you and learn from Me, for I am gentle and lowly in heart, and you will find rest for your souls. For My yoke is easy and My burden is light. (Matthew 11:28–30)

The Lord is not slack concerning His promise, as some count slackness, but is longsuffering toward us, not willing that any should perish but that all should come to repentance. (2 Peter 3:9)

Let us go right into the presence of God with sincere hearts fully trusting him. For our guilty consciences have been sprinkled with Christ's blood to make us clean, and our bodies have been washed with pure water. Let us hold tightly without wavering to the hope we affirm, for God can be trusted to keep his promise. (Hebrews 10:22–23 NLT)

For all of God's promises have been fulfilled in Christ with a resounding "Yes!" And through Christ, our "Amen" (which means "Yes") ascends to God for his glory. (2 Corinthians 1:20 NLT)

Fear not, for I have redeemed you; I have called you by your name; you are Mine. When you pass through the waters, I will be with you; and through the rivers, they shall not overflow you. When you walk through the fire, you shall not be burned, nor shall the flame scorch you. (Isaiah 43:1–2)

_____

_____

_____

BLESSINGS AND PROTECTION

May the LORD God of your fathers make you a thousand times more numerous than you are, and bless you as He has promised you! (Deuteronomy 1:11)

Many are the afflictions of the righteous, but the LORD delivers him out of them all. (Psalm 34:19)

Instead of shame and dishonor, you will enjoy a double share of honor. You will possess a double portion of prosperity in your land, and everlasting joy will be yours. (Isaiah 61:7 NLT)

The LORD bless you and keep you; the LORD make His face shine upon you, and be gracious to you; the LORD lift up His countenance upon you, and give you peace. (Numbers 6:24–26)

_____

_____

_____

18

PRAYERS FOR VETERANS

FREEDOM FROM GUILT:

Lord Jesus, please forgive me for the things that I did that were sinful and give me the grace to forgive myself, to be completely free from all the guilt and shame of my past. Thank You for giving me a whole new life, full of peace and joy. Amen.

FORGIVING THE GOVERNMENT (FOR LACK OF FINANCIAL SUPPORT OR NEEDED HEALTH CARE):

Father, help me forgive my country and its leaders for withholding from me the care I need for what I suffered as I served my country and its people. I choose to release them now from all bitterness and unforgiveness. I trust You to take care of me despite my difficult and sometimes desperate situation, because You died for me and You love me. Amen.

POVERTY:

Father, I thank You that the spirit of poverty is lifting off me, right now. I thank You that all of the financial problems I have suffered since I left the military are going away and that You are going to provide me with a good job and the income I need to have a future and a hope. I thank You that I will not be a stranger and an outcast in my own country, or full of anxiety and fear about my future, because You are watching over me and will meet my needs. Amen.

REJECTION:

Father, I curse all the traumas that have been stored in my body from abuse and the times I suffered rejection and command them to be removed from me. I thank You for releasing me from overreacting to daily events that tend to trigger the sense of rejection in me. I thank You that all these triggers are gone and all negative images, memories, or mental habit patterns be removed from my mind, right now, in Jesus's name. Amen.

SEXUAL ABUSE:

Father God, I command all the trauma stored in the cells of my body (cellular memory) as well as actual memory of the events to be totally erased and eliminated from my body, mind, and spirit. As a result of this rape/abuse, I was unwillingly made a covenant partner with my rapist/abuser. I ask You to release me from that unholy covenant and take away all the generational curses that entered into me at that time. Thank You, Lord Jesus, for totally cleansing my DNA and replacing the abuser's DNA in my body with Yours. I thank You for being the lover of my soul. Amen.

VERBAL ABUSE:

Father, I command all the experiences of verbal abuse that I have suffered over the years, and the trauma that stayed in my mind as a result of these episodes, to be removed from me forever. I thank You for cleaning out my ears with Holy Spirit Q-tips and replacing all of those word curses with Your love and blessings. I am free to give and receive words of kindness and love without rehearsing the word curses of the past. Amen.

CELLULAR MEMORY:

Lord, in Jesus's name, remove at the cellular level the horrific sights, the things seen, felt, and smelled. Remove the horrific things that have been done to me and the things I have had to do to others. Forgive me, Father. Remove any feelings of torment, pain, and anger from every cell in my body and mind. Fill my spirit with Yours. In Jesus's name. Amen.

DEPRESSION AND DEATH:

Father, in Jesus's name, I command the spirits of depression and death to lift off me. I speak life and health over my mind and spirit. I command all the evil that has been done to me and by others be gone. I thank You, Father, that my sins are forgiven and the sins that were done to me have been forgiven. I pray for a spirit of peace to rest upon my heart and mind. I pray that I will not look back to the memories of those traumatic experiences from the past. I will look forward to the future with confidence, knowing You have a good plan for my life. In Jesus's name. Amen.

SURVIVOR'S GUILT:

(This can develop from seeing or being involved in a traumatic event, such as seeing a friend die from war or a car accident. A person can feel at fault for the death or think they should have been the one who died.)

Father, I curse any kind of guilt, heaviness, or fault that developed by seeing a friend get hurt, lose a limb, or get killed. I lay that trauma and guilt on the altar. I release it all to You, including the memories of witnessing this event. Take all the bad memories from me. In Jesus's name. Amen.

PHYSICAL DISABILITY AS A RESULT OF SERVING:

Father, please forgive me for holding any unforgiveness toward the person who contributed to my pain and injury. I release any unforgiveness in Jesus's name. Fill me with Your love, joy, and peace in Jesus's name. Father, guide me into Your perfect plan for my life. Lead me to others I can help by sharing Your love. Thank You for being my Source for everything. I need to live for You. In Jesus's name. Amen.

PORNOGRAPHY:

(People come back from serving overseas and may turn to other things to dull their lingering pain. They may start with video games, which can be good in some instances. However, during their idle hours, some do nothing but watch TV, troll their computer, and perhaps accidentally find pornography. Soon, they have gotten hooked. While serving, men and women hardly breathe without orders from their commanding officer. Remember, God is the ultimate commanding officer. Everyone needs to look to Him for instructions and obey His Word and commands.)

Father, forgive me for that first glance at images I should have never looked at. I rebuke the spirit of addiction to pornography in Jesus's name. Father, remove those images from my memory immediately. Replace those images with Your love and joy. Lead me to healthy, productive activities within Your plan for my life. In Jesus's name. Amen.

19

STEPS TO FULFILLING
YOUR DESTINY

Recently, I was in a service and one of the ladies began to sing, "Great Is Thy Faithfulness." It was absolutely incredible and took us straight to the throne room. But as I sat there listening, I thought, "God, great *is* Thy faithfulness."

And I heard right back, "Great is *thy* faithfulness." I knew it was not only about God's faithfulness but ours. I knew many years ago that God had called me into the ministry, more than the work I was doing in the Dallas area. God was calling me to go out beyond co-pastoring a church, which I had done for eighteen years. Over and over, I heard God tell me, "Get ready. I'm going to send you out."

I knew God would send me all over the world. I just knew it! So I kept telling myself, *You have to be ready to go. God wants you ready for whatever He calls you to do.*

I began to prepare myself in the Spirit. I made sure I had a Bible all marked up exactly how I wanted it for preaching. I had my nails and hair done and even bought a new suit. I would be ready.

"Okay, God, I'm ready!" I said. "I've done everything that You told me to do. So where are You sending me?"

SENT OUT...TO GROCERY STORE

"I'm sending you to the grocery store," God said.

"Well, I was kind of hoping for Chicago or New York, God, but okay..." With four kids, I went to the grocery store on a regular basis. "Lord, that's the last place I want to go. But in Your Word, You say that if I'm faithful in little things, I'll rule over much."

God replied, "You've gone to the grocery store for all those years for yourself. Now I want you to go for *Me*."

Melody was still a young girl at the time, so I said, "Would you like to go to the grocery store with Mom?"

"Sure," she said.

So we went. Going down an aisle, I said, "Melody, what do you want for dinner tonight?... Melody? Melody?" I couldn't find her anywhere.

DAUGHTER FINDS PEOPLE IN NEED

Needless to say, I began to panic. Just then I heard, "Hey, Mom, come over to aisle three. This person has loss of hearing and we're going to pray for her healing!"

I hurried over to aisle three, laid hands on the person, and prayed, "In the name of Jesus, hearing be restored. Amen."

"Okay, Melody, what do you want for dinner tonight?... Melody!" She was gone again.

"Hey, Mom! Come over to aisle seven. Someone over here uses a cane and needs you to pray for them!"

I hurried over, prayed for the person, opened my eyes, and Melody was gone again.

To make a long story short, I never bought any groceries on that trip and we stopped for fast food on the way home. But I was faithful. As ridiculous as it seemed at the time, I went to the grocery store. And then God used me.

No matter how small of a job you think God has called you to do, you just need to do it! Be faithful in the little.

My motto is God will use your gift—no matter what it is. Whatever talent God has given you, use it faithfully.

FAITH YIELDS BLESSINGS

There's a woman who was fifteen when she went to work for my mom and dad many years ago. She was faithful to the call of the ministry. She worked all day long and did her school work in the evening. It took her longer to graduate than most because she only had a few hours a night for her education, but I'm sure she graduated with A's. She ran the office and the publishing company better than anybody has ever run it before or since.

She was faithful, even at fifteen years old—faithful in the little and God blessed her over and over. Be faithful in the little things and you will rule over much. God will give you an incredible vision of what you'll be doing.

The enemy will do whatever he can to keep you from accomplishing your vision. He wants to abort your dream and will stop at nothing. *"Recall the former days when, after you were enlightened, you endured a hard struggle with sufferings"* (Hebrews 10:32 ESV). Another translation puts it this way: *"Think back on those early days when you first learned about Christ. Remember how you remained faithful even though it meant terrible suffering"* (NLT).

You must be faithful—no matter what.

If you feel that God has revealed something you need to do, you've had no opposition, and the enemy hasn't tried to stop you, it's time to pray harder because it may not be of God. As Rick Renner has said, a spiritual fight usually occurs when you've been illuminated to the plan of God on your life.

CAN YOU PASS GOD'S TEST?

Sometimes, part of our testing is to prove our faithfulness to God *and* to ourselves. Are you willing, at all cost, to fulfill the call of God on your life? Don't try to escape the test. That time of testing is a proving ground. Just like basic training in the military, if you pass one test, you'll move up the ladder to a greater level of responsibility. It may not be easy and not everyone makes it. God wants us to pass the test and go on to a higher level with Him.

When Joseph reassured his brothers that he meant them no harm, he said, *"As for you, you meant evil against me; but God meant it for good, in order to bring it about as it is this day, to save many people alive"* (Genesis 50:20). God gave me this interpretation: "To minister to many and help them through their situation because you successfully made it through that same situation."

A CRISIS IS AN OPPORTUNITY

I have some friends in Houston, Tom and Amy. I called them the other day and said, "I need something written in Chinese," and explained what I wanted. They faxed it over. But the word *crisis* in Chinese is our word *together*. One character means potential danger; the other means hidden opportunity. Together, you have a crisis. In every situation that you go through, there's always potential danger, but there's also hidden opportunity.

I looked up *crisis* in the dictionary. It means a turning point, for better or worse. It could be a serious physical or spiritual disease that can result in recovery or death. Think of it not only in the natural, but in the Spirit. Another definition for crisis is change itself. Any kind of change can be a crisis. Your crisis is your birthplace for a miracle.

In Hebrew, the word *crisis* means *birthing chair* or *labor*, something no one can go through for you. You go through the travail of labor and birth a new life by yourself.

THE TRAVAIL OF CHILDBIRTH

During a meeting, I asked a friend to come up front for a moment. Then I said, "I want you to tell me what it was like, personally, to give birth to your daughter, Rebecca."

"I have no idea," he said.

"Why not?" I asked.

"Because I didn't give birth to my child."

"But you were there."

"I was a witness," he said.

"I was there too," I replied.

"You helped deliver Rebecca," he said.

"Yes, I did," I said. "Rebecca was stuck and I helped her out. Then I hollered for you to come in and cut the cord."

"And I cut the cord," Adrian said.

Yes, my friend cuts hair and he cut the cord. And yet, his wife had a totally different experience birthing their daughter than either of us did.

Because I have birthed four children, I can tell you what that's like. I can also tell you what it's like to go through a divorce, be diagnosed with breast cancer, be co-dependent, and lose all of your income and financial support from an ex-husband and have nothing. But I can also tell you how God met my every need! I'd just as soon not have had those personal experiences and yet God got me through them.

LET GOD TEACH YOU

Whatever you're going through right now, allow God to teach you in every area so that you will learn, not only for your sake, but for others. You'll be able to minister and save the lives around you. Yes, your situation was meant for harm; yes, it was meant to kill you. Allow God to use it. Pray, "God, send me what I need to learn during this time because I want to get through it."

"Yea, though I walk through the valley of the shadow of death, I will fear no evil" (Psalm 23:4). Praise the Lord, you don't stay there, you only walk *through*

it. Unfortunately, too many people just stay. You have to get up and go on with what God's called you to do.

I recently went to the garden of Gethsemane in Israel to pray. I could feel the very presence of God there. Two thousand years ago, Jesus prayed there in agony because He knew what would happen over the next few days: the crown of thorns, the beatings, the shouted lies, the humiliation, the cross, the spear in His side—everything. Don't you think He had a mental struggle over the call of God on His life?

JESUS SUBMITTED HIMSELF

Jesus had a battle between what His flesh wanted and what His Father wanted. He said, *"Father, if it is Your will, take this cup away from Me; nevertheless not My will, but Yours, be done"* (Luke 22:42). Jesus submitted His will to the call of God on His life. *"Then an angel appeared to Him from heaven, strengthening Him. And being in agony, He prayed more earnestly. Then His sweat became like great drops of blood falling down to the ground"* (Luke 22:43–44). When we submit our will to God, an angel of the Lord will strengthen us beyond words, beyond measure.

Jesus was so stressed out that He began to sweat. Not just a little perspiration, but drops of blood. I've been under a lot of stress, but never to the point where I have sweat blood. However, I have been through the anguish of, "God, I don't want to do this. I don't want to endure that pain. I don't want…"

Yet Jesus said, "I submit; *You* know why I need to go through this." As a result, He made a way for us to get into heaven.

Daniel 11:32 says, *"The people who know their God shall be strong, and carry out great exploits."* Don't just stay where you are. Those who know their God will be strong and resist the devil. Take the situation you've either gone through or face now and use it to make you stronger than you've ever been before. And do you know what will happen? You will do great exploits for your Commander in Chief, Almighty God.

> *Do not think it strange concerning the fiery trial which is to try you, as though some strange thing happened to you; but rejoice to the extent that you partake of Christ's sufferings, that when His glory is revealed, you may also be glad with exceeding joy…. Therefore let those who suffer according to the will of God commit their souls to Him in doing good, as to a faithful Creator.* (1 Peter 4:12–13, 19)

UNWAVERING FAITH IN GOD

While I was on a plane a few years ago, God laid it on my heart to share part of my testimony with the flight attendant. Afterward, she said, "Your story sounds like mine." Then she looked at me and asked, "Did your faith in God ever waver?"

"No," I replied.

"I got really mad at God once, rebelled, and walked away from Him," she said. "Have you ever walked away from God?"

"No," I shook my head.

"Well, did you want to curse God?"

"No."

"You didn't?" she said. "Really? I don't know how you went through all that and didn't just turn your back on God." She just couldn't imagine it not affecting me that way.

"God's the one that got me through it," I explained. "It made me stronger in the Lord than ever before." We talked a little longer. And that flight attendant has since rededicated her life and gone back to church.

When you're willing and open, you never know where God will call you or what He'll ask you to do. Be faithful!

THE BEST OPTION IS GOD

Recently, someone said to me, "I think now would be a good time to drink away your troubles." She added, "But due to the fact that you don't drink, that's just not an option." We laughed.

When you're in a crisis, it's so easy to go to the bottle, drugs, or food. Or you can go to the cross. The choice is yours. Unfortunately, too many people make the wrong choice. Outside elements are only a temporary fix. One day, you'll come out of your stupor and reality will hit you again. So you might as well just deal with the reality, go to the cross, and lay it at Jesus's feet. He will help you go through it and get on with your life.

Finally, my brethren, be strong in the Lord and in the power of His might. Put on the whole armor of God, that you may be able to stand against the wiles of the devil. For we do not wrestle against flesh and blood, but against principalities, against powers, against the rulers of the darkness of this age, against spiritual hosts of wickedness in the heavenly places. Therefore take up the whole armor of God, that you may be able to withstand in the evil day, and having done all, to stand. Stand therefore, having girded your waist with truth, having put on the breastplate of righteousness, and having shod your feet with the preparation of the gospel of peace; above all, taking the shield of faith with which you will be able to quench all the fiery darts of the wicked one. And take the helmet of salvation, and the sword of the Spirit, which is the word of God.   (Ephesians 6:10–17)

WEAR THE WHOLE ARMOR OF GOD

Put on the *whole* armor of God, not just the helmet of salvation to protect your mind and keep it centered on Jesus Christ. Think about the guys in Iraq, Afghanistan, or elsewhere. What would happen if they had no clothes or uniform and no weapons, just a helmet? They'd be killed very quickly.

So many times, Christians put on the helmet of salvation, but where's the breastplate of righteousness to protect their heart? Where's the shield of faith to block Satan's attacks? We need the whole armor of God to be able to live a sanctified life, set apart in the world, but not of the world.

When my daughters were young, I dressed them. But now, they are adults and can dress themselves and make their own choices. And so can you. Take off the old man, put on the new man, and go out and do what God's called you to do. I took off the old man and put on the new man when I was twelve, so God saved me from a life of drinking, smoking, and cussing.

You had uniforms to put on while you were in the service—a dress uniform, everyday uniform, and perhaps camouflage khakis. Now you need to put on the armor of God, His uniform. Wear the full armor of God to make it through these end times. Remember, even the words you speak become part of your armor. Praise surrounds you with God's protection.

GOING ON THE OFFENSIVE

Read those verses from Ephesians again. Notice that the armor of God is on the front with the back exposed? That's because we're on the offensive and not running from the enemy. God always sends His people to stand in the gap and guard our back.

When I was in Israel, I met several members of the Israeli army. I learned that they sleep with their boots on and one hand on their weapon. They're prepared for attack around the clock.

We too need to be prepared at all times to go to war, no matter what the enemy tries to throw at us. Jesus told his followers, *"The kingdom of heaven suffers violence, and the violent take it by force"* (Matthew 11:12). You can sit back and allow the enemy to walk all over you, or you can get up, be forceful, and take on the kingdom of God. Walk out the calling of God on your life. No one can make that choice for you. It's up to you.

Can you imagine what happened when Lakewood Church found out that their founding pastor, John Osteen, had died? So many people thought that Lakewood would die, too, but God raised up someone who had directed the programs for twenty years. Joel had never preached a sermon until the Sunday before his dad died and God placed him in the pulpit. Lakewood Church has since grown to one of the largest churches in America.

GOD CAN USE YOU IN A MIGHTY WAY

Take the time to prepare for what God is getting ready to do in and through you.

When Joseph was a teenager, he was taken to Egypt as a slave. Because he was faithful to God in all that he did, God used him to save his family from a horrible famine. In Genesis 41:52, Joseph says, *"God has caused me to be fruitful in the land of my affliction."*

No matter what troubles and trials come your way, allow God to use you. If you'll let Him, He will use you in a mighty way.

Here are some other Scriptures to keep in mind:

But thanks be to God, who gives us the victory through our Lord Jesus Christ. Therefore, my beloved brethren, be steadfast, immovable, always abounding in the work of the Lord, knowing that your labor is not in vain in the Lord. (1 Corinthians 15:57–58)

Yet in all these things we are more than conquerors through Him who loved us. For I am persuaded that neither death nor life, nor angels nor principalities nor powers, nor things present nor things to come, nor height nor depth, nor any other created thing, shall be able to separate us from the love of God which is in Christ Jesus our Lord. (Romans 8:37–39)

Be merciful to me, O God, be merciful to me! For my soul trusts in You; and in the shadow of Your wings I will make my refuge, until these calamities have passed by. (Psalm 57:1)

GOD WILL NOT FORSAKE YOU

Moses told Joshua in front of all the people of Israel, *"Be strong and of good courage, for you must go with this people to the land which the* LORD *has sworn to their fathers to give them, and you shall cause them to inherit it. And the* LORD, *He is the One who goes before you. He will be with you, He will not leave you nor forsake you; do not fear nor be dismayed"* (Deuteronomy 31:7–8).

God promises never to leave me nor forsake me and He promises to always support me, whether it's emotionally, physically, or financially. And He will do the same for *you*.

God told me, "I'm taking you to a higher level. I'm giving you a greater understanding of the pain that you've been through and you're going to walk it out. So line up with Me and get ready."

God will raise you up and take you to a higher level in a lot of areas, but primarily in giving you a heart of compassion to minister to our world. God will work through your hands, your mouth, and your heart to help others who are desperate for the right answers. Be that conduit and reach out!

There is nothing too hard for God. He tells us, "I can do a better job than you. You're just prolonging things. Let Me handle it for you."

God said to me, "I'm preparing to reward your faithfulness beyond measure." And I saw the windows of heaven opening up. I believe that's a word for you, too. I pray:

Father, I praise and thank You for Your Word. I speak a greater determination in the heart, mind, soul, and body of every person who is reading this. Whatever has kept them from doing what You've called them to do, whether it's sickness, inadequacy, low self-esteem, or even if they feel like their marriage partner has kept them from doing Your will, I thank You that they will overcome every single one of those. I command that their gifts be stirred up within them and that their eyes of understanding be enlightened to all that You have for them.

Father, I thank You that they will walk in the supernatural and are entering the Holy of Holies where your Shekinah glory lights their way. Father, we thank You for the gifts and the fruit of the Spirit, that they may walk in them. I thank You for Your wisdom and guidance in what they are to do. In Jesus's name. Amen.

A HEALING PRAYER

If you're reading this and still need healing, please pray out loud:

Father, You know my needs. In the name of Jesus, I speak total healing from the top of my head to the soles of my feet. For the electrical, chemical, and hormonal frequencies to become in harmony and balance. Get rid of every bad cell and guide the blood flowing through me.

I speak emotional healing to my mind and heart. And I speak restoration of everything that the devil has stolen in my life, physical, emotional, spiritual, and financial. I speak a breakthrough in every area.

Father, You have provided for me and sustained me. And I curse any form of stress in my life. Your Word says that You give Your beloved sweet sleep at the right time. And I thank You for giving me better sleep than I have ever had before, greater peace than ever before.

Father, I thank You that You are renewing my mind, heart, body, spirit, and strength. Thank You for filling me so that I can fulfill Your call upon my life.

Father, I thank You that Your Word says that You not only want us healed but You want us whole. I speak wholeness right now, in Jesus's name. Father, I give You all the glory. In Jesus's name. Amen.

God says, "For I have taken you through a time of stretching, of greater appreciation, and of greater learning. I have stretched you beyond what you thought possible. But your time of stress is coming to a close."

I speak this blessing over you:

Now may the God of peace who brought up our Lord Jesus from the dead, that great Shepherd of the sheep, through the blood of the everlasting covenant, make you complete in every good work to do His will, working in you what is well pleasing in His sight, through Jesus Christ, to whom be glory forever and ever. Amen. (Hebrews 13:20–21)

20

A BUCKET LIST

If you could do anything in the world before you die, what would it be? Make a list of all the things you have thought about doing. Some people call this their bucket list. You can call it whatever you'd like.

It is time you worked toward those dreams. God gives you those dreams and the means with which to accomplish them. Choose just one thing every day and do something toward a goal. Maybe you want to work on one thing each week. You decide.

Maybe you want to do some research on the Internet. If you don't have a computer accessible, go to your local library. They can get you started. Check your local community for classes or seminars. Many classes are free if you don't need credits toward a degree or certification. The Internet offers endless instruction on most subjects. Get busy!

Since God has brought you safely through your past and all those challenges, just know that the call of God on your life will always remain there. The important thing is, what will you do with it? You may ignore it, you may talk yourself out of it, people may try to talk you out of it, or circumstances and opportunities may distract you right out of the will of God. Opportunities will come and they will go, but what you do with them makes a difference. It is so important that you follow the voice of God and do what He calls you to do.

> *But as for you, you meant evil against me; but God meant it for good, in order to bring it about as it is this day, to save many people alive.*
>
> (Genesis 50:20)

Once you understand this verse, you'll also realize that God can use your situation for His glory. The enemy has been setting up plans for our destruction...yours and mine. That is his job. He meant my past for evil, but I wouldn't allow his advance on my position. I took it, turned it around, and made a miracle out of it. I chose to make the devil sorry he ever did or tried to do anything to me.

There are many opportunities to overcome in life. I have bounced out of potholes. I've been pushed into deep, dark caves. But I couldn't let any attack destroy me! I had to fill up the potholes, crawl out of the caves, and keep going. And so do you.

DON'T GIVE UP—GOD HASN'T

God gave each one of us free will to make our own choices. You may feel your life is no longer productive or worthwhile. Well, guess again! God has guided you through every step of your journey and He hasn't given up on you yet. He has many exciting adventures waiting for your future.

Your previous chapter has come to a close. It's time to start the next chapter of your life. Happiness, joy, peace, and excitement are waiting for you. His provision is waiting for you to receive, pick up, and run. New learning experiences will push you up another step of the ladder. None of us has graduated yet. Keep climbing!

Study the life of David in the Bible. Even though he was hardly perfect, God forgave his mistakes and made him one of the greatest kings ever known to man. However, if you look at his past, you'll realize he had a bumpy road of sin before getting on God's path for his life. He was guilty of adultery and murder. (See 2 Samuel 11.) Remember, this is the same man recorded in the Bible as "a man after God's own heart." (See 1 Samuel 13:14; Acts 13:22.) God took that situation, turned it around, and made a miracle out of it. David had a heart transformation. He sought the heart of God.

We all need to have a heart transformation. What does that mean? David wanted the heart of God and His calling on his life. At the end of his life, David didn't have to look back and say, "I coulda shoulda done..." *He had the heart of God.*

Moses is another awesome man of God. He rescued a Hebrew slave who was being beaten and stood up for the daughters of Jethro, the priest of Midian, when some shepherds chased them away from the well. (See Exodus 2:11–17.)

God wanted Moses to lead the Israelites out of Egypt, but even after seeing the Lord's miracles, Moses told God, *"O my Lord, I am not eloquent neither before nor since You have spoken to Your servant; but I am slow of speech and slow of tongue"* (Exodus 4:10).

Whine, whine, whine! God called him and was equipping him, but in his natural mind, Moses didn't believe God could use him. He felt he would be an embarrassment to the Lord.

God said, "I've called you—I'll qualify you."

Moses replied, "Oh, my Lord, please use somebody else, not me." Yet God used him in a miraculous way to lead the Israelites to freedom.

GOD WILL WORK THINGS OUT

If God calls you to do something, He will work things out so you can accomplish His will for your life.

Twenty years ago, if you had told me I would have twenty published books, a TV show, and a worldwide ministry that had me traveling everywhere to teach others how to be healed physically, spiritually, mentally, and financially, I would have said, "You're crazy."

When God called me, my reaction was, "I can't do that. The world says I'm dumb, stupid, ignorant, and slow, that I can't read and can't write. I was told I'd never, ever be used of God." And I believed that for most of my life.

I could easily have said, "God, I can't," but I was reminded in the Word of God that *"I can do all things through Christ who strengthens me"* (Philippians 4:13).

Sometimes, people go after their dream with the greatest of intentions. When obstacles pop up, they quit and go home. I have little signs around my house and office that say, "Never, never, never, never give up. Go under, go over, go through, but never give up." I'm a no-matter-what kind of a woman—and God wants you to believe the same thing.

GOD CAN USE YOU IN MIGHTY WAYS

Understand this: God wants to forgive everyone when they truly repent for their negative behaviors. Once you repent and accept Him as your Father, God can use you in mighty ways.

Read about other people in the Bible who did great things once they turned their lives over to God—people like Ruth, Esther, Daniel, Timothy, Peter, and Paul. They were hardly perfect and they are great examples of how God can turn a life around.

Paul was a devout Jew who persecuted and killed Christians until he encountered Jesus on the Damascus Road. (See Acts 9.) And his life was forever changed.

Paul had to get out of his comfort zone in order to be an effective follower of Christ. People can be healed, set free, and called of God. However, leaving our comfort zone to pray for other people can be a little overwhelming. God took this man with a violent past and used him in amazing ways to further His kingdom and spread the gospel throughout the known world.

I've talked about various people who were willing to sacrifice their life to be used of God. Are you willing to give your life to God so He can use you, too? Are you ready to use your previous experiences to advance you into the next powerful phase of your life? Are you ready to fight today's battle and help your brothers and sisters in arms to reach total victory?

How can I, Joan Hunter, travel the world? God gave me a plan. How can you do what He's called you to do? God will give *you* a plan.

LOOK AHEAD, NOT BEHIND

Many years ago, I worked at a car dealership, an amazing company out of the Dallas-Fort Worth area. The dealership also did a lot of body work. One day, I asked, "May I have a rearview mirror?" They had lots of them in the body shop, so they said, "Sure."

I used that mirror to demonstrate a very important principle. Every car has a rearview mirror as a safety device. But if you constantly look at what's behind you while you drive down the road, you will definitely run into something ahead of you.

Often, people concentrate on their past instead of focusing on their future. They continually live in the past, thinking of all the things they *should* have done. They may believe they let God down, denied Christ, and slipped into unforgivable sin. They believe there is no way that God would ever forgive or use them.

There is nothing wrong with thinking about your past and learning from previous experiences, but God wants you to focus on your future. He has great things ahead of you. (See Jeremiah 29:11; Romans 8:18.) Step into His best life, which is right ahead. Don't focus on your life's rearview mirror. Look for His best coming in front of you. Miracles are passing you by. Reach out and grab what is meant just for you.

Looking back on my life, I know I am not the same person today that I was in times past. I look at my future and think, *I'm a woman after God's own heart. God, use me for Your purposes today and every day. I belong to You. I will follow You.*

ASK GOD FOR GUIDANCE

Rise up and meet the call of God on your life. God must get very tired of hearing excuses. God wants you to start off your day speaking to Him and asking for His guidance. He wants you to wake up every morning with an attitude of obedience. He is your Commander in Chief and you are a member of His troops on the ground. You must follow His orders and use what you have been trained to do to advance toward ultimate victory.

What has God called *you* to do? It's so important that you understand the call of God on your life.

TOSS EXCUSES AWAY

What are you confessing out of your mouth? God will never use me because…

…I'm too old

…I'm too young

…I'm too fat

…I'm too skinny

…I'm married

…I'm single

…I have children

…I have no kids

Throw all those excuses right out the window and don't pick them up again! God just wants to use you, if you're willing. And if you let Him, your life will be an amazing journey.

PRAY FOR GOD TO USE YOU

God uses me in incredible ways around the world. Yes, I minister to people in meetings and seminars, but I also can anonymously pray for people in the grocery store, a super store, an airport, or anywhere else He sends me. God heals others through me and He can do the same for you. Let Him use you to do His work. Your hands become His hands. Your words come from Him. Make sure whoever you pray for knows that the precious name of Jesus is healing them, not your human hands. They don't even need to know your name.

Be willing. Simply say, "God, use me. I repent for my excuses. I repent for denying Your power through me. I don't want to regret missing an opportunity to allow You to work through me to help others. I want to live a life of no regrets from this moment on."

THE GOOD NEWS OF SALVATION

The following verses have been the basis for my ministry since the beginning:

> *The Spirit of the Lord GOD is upon Me, because the LORD has anointed Me to preach good tidings to the poor; He has sent Me to heal the broken-hearted, to proclaim liberty to the captives, and the opening of the prison to those who are bound; to proclaim the acceptable year of the LORD, and the day of vengeance of our God; to comfort all who mourn, to console those who mourn in Zion, to give them beauty for ashes, the oil of joy for mourning, the garment of praise for the spirit of heaviness; that they may be called trees of righteousness, the planting of the LORD, that He may be glorified.* (Isaiah 61:1–3)

I challenge you to read these verses, remember them, and stand on them for your future. You will find them very powerful as He sends you out with His direction and anointing to work in His kingdom on earth. I advise you to read the entire chapter of Isaiah 61, which is entitled "The Good News of Salvation" for a reason. It is awe-inspiring to say the least.

Get ready! God will use you in a mighty way.

RESOURCES

Anxiety and Depression Association of America

adaa.org
8701 Georgia Ave., Suite 412
Silver Spring, MD 20910
240-485-1001

Founded in 1979, the Anxiety and Depression Association of America (ADAA) is an international nonprofit organization dedicated to the prevention, treatment, and cure of anxiety, depression, OCD, PTSD, and co-occurring disorders through education, practice, and research.

Building Homes for Heroes

www.buildinghomesforheroes.org
4584 Austin Blvd.
Island Park, NY 11558
516-684-9220

Building Homes for Heroes is a nationwide partnership of communities and corporations committed to rebuilding lives and supporting the servicemen and women who served during the wars in Iraq or Afghanistan. The organization builds or modifies homes, and gifts them, mortgage-free, to veterans and their families.

Department of Veterans Affairs

www.va.gov
1722 I St. NW
Washington, DC 20421
800-827-1000

The Department of Veterans Affairs strives to fulfill President Lincoln's promise to serve and honor veterans and their surviving spouses and children.

Disabled American Veterans

www.dav.org
3725 Alexandria Pike
Cold Spring, KY 41076
877-426-2838

DAV is a nonprofit charity that provides a lifetime of support for veterans of all generations and their families, helping more than one million veterans each year.

Equine Assisted Growth and Learning Association

www.eagala.org
P.O. Box 246
Spanish Fork, UT 84660
801-754-0400

Eagala (Equine Assisted Growth and Learning Association) is a network offering equine-assisted therapy, including a program designed specifically for veterans.

HelpGuide

www.helpguide.org
1250 6th Street, Suite 400
Santa Monica, CA 90401

HelpGuide is a mental health and wellness website with the mission of providing empowering, evidence-based information on PTSD, trauma, and other issues.

Homes For Our Troops

www.hfotusa.org
6 Main Street
Taunton, MA 02780
866-787-6677

Homes For Our Troops builds and donates specially adapted custom homes nationwide for severely injured post-9/11 veterans.

Hope for Heroes Foundation

heroeshope.org
P.O. Box 152
Billings, NY 12510
845-476-9142

Hope for Heroes helps disabled heroes heal and feel a sense of personal accomplishment, empowerment, and unity with other veterans through outdoor activities such as hunting, deep-sea fishing, boating, hiking, and camping.

Joan Hunter Ministries

joanhunter.org
P.O. Box 111
Tomball, TX 77377
281-789-7500

Joan offers many healing prayers, appropriate Scriptures, and the opportunity to have someone pray with you. Leave your prayer request online or call to talk to one of the ministers.

Lone Survivor Foundation

lonesurvivorfoundation.org
1414 11th St., Suite 1
Huntsville, TX 77340
936-755-6075

Lone Survivor Foundation restores, empowers, and renews hope for wounded service members, veterans, and their families through health, wellness, and therapeutic support.

Make the Connection

maketheconnection.net

Make the Connection is an online resource offered through the U.S. Department of Veterans Affairs that's designed to connect veterans, their family members and friends, and other supporters with information, resources, and solutions to issues affecting their lives.

Merging Vets & Players

www.vetsandplayers.org
8225 Sunset Blvd.
West Hollywood, CA 90046
323-536-9322

Merging Vets & Players' mission is to match up combat veterans and former professional athletes to give them a new team to tackle the transition to a new life together and show them they are not alone.

Mental Health America

www.mhanational.org
500 Montgomery St., Suite 820
Alexandria, VA 22314
703-684-7722; 800-969-6642

Mental Health America is a community-based nonprofit dedicated to addressing the needs of those living with mental illness and promoting the overall mental health of all Americans.

Mighty Oaks Foundation

www.mightyoaksprograms.org
29910 Murrieta Hot Springs Rd. Ste. G530
Murrieta, CA 92563
951-240-3011

The Mighty Oaks Foundation serves the military community with peer-to-peer, faith-based, combat-trauma recovery programs and combat-resiliency conferences, held at multiple locations nationwide.

Military OneSource

www.militaryonesource.mil
800-342-9647 (confidential help line)

Military OneSource from the U.S. Department of Defense aims to be a one-stop, online resource of information for active duty personnel.

National Center for PTSD

www.ptsd.va.gov

Part of the U.S. Department of Veterans Affairs, the center's goal is to be the world's leading research and educational center of excellence on PTSD and traumatic stress.

National Coalition for Homeless Veterans

www.nchv.org
1730 M St. NW, Suite 705
Washington, DC 20036
800-838-4357

The National Coalition for Homeless Veterans is a resource and technical assistance center for a national network of community-based service providers and local, state, and federal agencies that provide housing, employment services, case management, legal aid, and other supportive services each year to thousands of veterans experiencing or at-risk of homelessness.

National Resource Directory

nrd.gov
800-342-9647 (programs)
800-827-1000 (benefits)

Offered by the federal government, the National Resource Directory is an online partnership for wounded, ill, and injured service members, veterans, their families, and those who support them.

National Veterans Foundation

nvf.org
5777 West Century Blvd., Suite 350
Los Angeles, CA 90045
310-642-0255
Vet to Vet Assistance: 888-777-4443

The National Veterans Foundation helps veterans and their families who are enduring a crisis or who have a critical need for help. Its goal is to serve the crisis management, information, and referral needs of all U.S. veterans and their families through management and operation of the nation's first vet-to-vet, toll-free helpline, public awareness programs, and outreach services.

Operation Homefront

www.operationhomefront.org
1355 Central Parkway S, Ste. 100
San Antonio, TX 78232
800-722-6098

Operation Homefront's mission is to build strong, stable, and secure military families so they can thrive in the communities that they've worked so hard to protect. It offers a Transitional Homes for Community Reintegration housing program to help veterans and their families transition from a military to a civilian community.

Paralyzed Veterans of America

www.pva.org
801 18th Street NW
Washington, DC 20006-3517
800-424-8200

Paralyzed Veterans of America is dedicated to serving veterans and supporting medical research, advocacy, and civil rights for all people with disabilities.

Stop Soldier Suicide

stopsoldiersuicide.org
P.O. Box 110605
Durham, NC 27709
844-889-5610

Stop Soldier Suicide is a national, veteran-led organization focused on military suicide prevention. Founded by three U.S. Army veterans who witnessed the military suicide crisis firsthand, it provides support and resources to all service members, veterans, and military families from every branch and every generation, regardless of discharge status.

Team Red, White & Blue

www.teamrwb.org
5428 Eisenhower Ave.
Alexandria, VA 22304
571-982-5173

Team Red, White & Blue aims to enrich the lives of America's veterans by connecting them to their community through physical and social activity.

Veterans Crisis Line

www.veteranscrisisline.net
1-800-273-8255, press 1; text 838255

The Veterans Crisis Line is a free, confidential resource that's available to all veterans, current service members, members of the National Guard or Reserve, family members, and friends. The responders are specially trained and experienced in helping people of all ages and circumstances. The resource is available 24/7.

Veterans' Families United Foundation

veteransfamiliesunited.org
P.O. Box 14355
Oklahoma City, OK 73113
405-535-1925

Veterans' Families United is an all-volunteer organization whose mission is to provide gentle, accessible, and holistic healing resources for veterans. It provides information on a wide variety of topics and hundreds of links to useful websites.

Veterans of Foreign Wars

www.vfw.org
VFW National Headquarters
406 W. 34th St.
Kansas City, Missouri 64111
816-756-3390

The Veterans of Foreign Wars is a nonprofit veterans' service organization comprised of eligible veterans and military service members from the active, guard, and reserve forces. Its mission is to foster camaraderie among United States veterans of overseas conflicts; serve veterans, the military, and our communities; and to advocate on behalf of all veterans.

Volunteers of America

www.voa.org/veterans
1660 Duke St.
Alexandria, VA 22314
703-341-5000

Volunteers of America calls itself "a church without walls." Nearly 16,000 paid professional employees and approximately 60,000 volunteers throughout the country help those in need rebuild their lives and reach their full potential. Nearly 1.5 million people are helped each year. The organization offers hundreds of human service programs, including some specifically for veterans.

We Honor Veterans

www.wehonorveterans.org
NHPCO
1731 King St.
Alexandria, VA 22314
703-837-1500

We Honor Veterans is a program of the National Hospice and Palliative Care Organization (NHPCO) in collaboration with the U.S. Department of Veterans Affairs. It teams up hospices and VA facilities to serve veterans and their families.

Wounded Warrior Project

www.woundedwarriorproject.org
4899 Belfort Road, Suite 300
Jacksonville, FL 32256
877-832-6997

Wounded Warrior Project specifically helps veterans and service members who incurred a physical or mental injury, illness, or wound while serving in the military on or after September 11, 2001.

ABOUT THE AUTHOR

Joan Hunter is a compassionate minister, dynamic teacher, accomplished author, and anointed healing evangelist who has devoted her life to carrying a message of hope, deliverance, and healing to the nations. As founder and president of Joan Hunter Ministries, Hearts 4 Him, and 4 Corners Conference Center, and president of Hunter Ministries, Joan has a vision to equip believers to take the healing power of God beyond the four walls of the church to the four corners of the earth. Joan's genuine approach and candid delivery enables her to connect intimately with people from all walks of life. Some describe her as "Carol Burnett with the anointing of Jesus."

Joan ministers the gospel with manifestations of supernatural signs and wonders in healing schools, miracle services, conferences, churches, and revival centers around the world. She is sensitive to the move of the Spirit and speaks prophetically to the local body and into the individual lives of those in attendance. Joan's genuine approach and candid delivery enable her to connect intimately with people from all educational, social, and cultural backgrounds.

At the age of twelve, Joan committed her life to Christ and began faithfully serving in ministry alongside her parents, Charles and Frances Hunter, as they traveled around the globe conducting healing explosions and healing schools until their deaths. Prior to branching out into her own international healing ministry, Joan also co-pastored a church for eighteen years.

Joan brings a powerful ministry to a world characterized by brokenness and pain. Having emerged victorious through tragic circumstances, impossible obstacles, and immeasurable devastation, Joan is able to share a message of hope and restoration to the brokenhearted, deliverance and freedom to the bound, and healing and wholeness to the diseased. Joan's life is one of uncompromising dedication to the gospel of Jesus Christ, as she exhibits a sincere desire to see the body of Christ live in freedom, happiness, wholeness, and financial wellness.

Joan has ministered in countries all over the world and has been featured on *Sid Roth's It's Supernatural*, *My New Day* with Drs. Bob and Audrey Meisner, *Everlasting Love* with Patricia King, and on Marilyn Hickey's *Today with Marilyn and Sarah*. Joan hosts a powerful and exciting show of her own, *Miracles Happen!* Joan's television appearances have been broadcast around the world on World Harvest Network, Inspiration Network, Daystar, Faith TV, Cornerstone TV, The Church Channel, Total Christian Television, Christian Television Network, Victory Television Network, Watchmen Broadcasting, and God TV. Joan also has her own channel on Roku.

She is a noted author whose books include *Love Again, Live Again*; *Healing the Whole Man Handbook*; *Healing the Heart*; *Power to Heal*; *Supernatural Provision*; *Freedom Beyond Comprehension*; and *Miracle Maintenance*.

Joan and her husband, Kelley, live northwest of Houston, Texas. Together, they have four grown children and a number of grandchildren.